2nd Workshop on Sentiment Analysis Where AI Meets Psychology

(SAAIP 2012)

Held at the 24th International Conference on Computational Linguistics (COLING 2012)

Mumbai, India
15 December 2012

Editors:

Sivaji Bandyopadhyay
Manabu Okumura

ISBN: 978-1-62748-354-4

Printed from e-media with permission by:

Curran Associates, Inc.
57 Morehouse Lane
Red Hook, NY 12571

CURRAN ASSOCIATES INC. proceedings.com

Some format issues inherent in the e-media version may also appear in this print version.

Printed by Curran Associates, Inc. (2013)

Association for Computational Linguistics
209 N. Eighth Street
Stroudsburg, Pennsylvania 18360

Phone: 1-570-476-8006
Fax: 1-570-476-0860

acl@aclweb.org

Additional copies of this publication are available from:

Curran Associates, Inc.
57 Morehouse Lane
Red Hook, NY 12571 USA
Phone: 845-758-0400
Fax: 845-758-2634
Email: curran@proceedings.com
Web: www.proceedings.com

COLING 2012

24th International Conference on Computational Linguistics

Proceedings of the 2nd Workshop on Sentiment Analysis where AI meets Psychology (SAAIP 2012)

Workshop chairs:
Sivaji Bandyopadhyay and Manabu Okumura

15 December 2012
Mumbai, India

Diamond sponsors

Tata Consultancy Services
Linguistic Data Consortium for Indian Languages (LDC-IL)

Gold Sponsors

Microsoft Research
Beijing Baidu Netcon Science Technology Co. Ltd.

Silver sponsors

IBM, India Private Limited
Crimson Interactive Pvt. Ltd.
Yahoo
Easy Transcription & Software Pvt. Ltd.

Preface

In recent times, research activities in the areas of Opinion, Sentiment and/or Emotion in natural language texts and other media are gaining ground under the umbrella of affect computing. Huge amount of text data are available in the Social Web in the form of news, reviews, blogs, chats and even twitter. Sentiment analysis from natural language text is a multifaceted and multidisciplinary problem. The existing reported solutions or available systems are still far from perfect or fail to meet the satisfaction level of the end users. There are many conceptual rules that govern sentiment and there are even more clues (possibly unlimited) that can map these concepts from realization to verbalization of a human being. Human psychology that relates to social, cultural, behavioral and environmental aspects of civilization may provide the unrevealed clues and govern the sentiment realization. In the present scenario we need constant research endeavors to reveal and incorporate the human psychological knowledge into machines in the best possible ways. The important issues that need attention include how various psychological phenomena can be explained in computational terms and the various artificial intelligence (AI) concepts and computer modeling methodologies that are most useful from the psychologist's point of view.

Regular research papers on sentiment analysis continue to be published in reputed conferences like ACL, EACL, NAACL, EMNLP or COLING. The Sentiment Analysis Symposiums are also drawing the attention of the research communities from every nook and corner of the world. There has been an increasing number of efforts in shared tasks such as SemEval 2007 Task#14: Affective Text, SemEval 2013 Task#14:Sentiment Analysis on Twitter, TAC 2008 Opinion Summarization task, TREC-BLOG tracks since 2006 and relevant NTCIR tracks since 6th NTCIR that have aimed to focus on different issues of opinion and emotion analysis. Several communities from sentiment analysis have engaged themselves to conduct relevant conferences, e.g., Affective Computing and Intelligent Interfaces (ACII) in 2009 and 2011 and workshops such as "Sentiment and Subjectivity in Text" in COLING-ACL 2006, "Sentiment Analysis – Emotion, Metaphor, Ontology and Terminology (EMOT)" in LREC 2008, Opinion Mining and Sentiment Analysis (WOMSA) 2009, "Topic-Sentiment Analysis for Mass Opinion Measurement (TSA)" in CIKM 2009, "Computational Approaches to Analysis and Generation of Emotion in Text" in NAACL 2010, Workshop on Computational Approaches to Subjectivity and Sentiment Analysis (WASSA) in ECAI 2010, ACL 2011 and ACL 2012, FLAIRS 2011 special track on "Affect Computing", Sentiment Elicitation from Natural Text for Information Retrieval and Extraction (SENTIRE 2011 and SENTIRE 2012), EMOTION SENTIMENT & SOCIAL SIGNALS (ES^3 2012) in the satellite of LREC 2012, Practice and Theory of Opinion Mining and Sentiment Analysis in conjunction with KONVENS-2012 (PATHOS-2012), Workshop on Intelligent Approaches applied to Sentiment Mining and Emotion Analysis **(**WISMEA, 2012**)**, Workshop on "Issues of Sentiment Discovery and Opinion Mining (WISDOM, 2012) and a bunch of special sessions like Sentiment Analysis for Asian Languages (SAAL, 2012), Brain Inspired Natural Language Processing (BINLP, 2012), Advances in Cognitive and Emotional Information Processing (ACEIP, 2012) and so on.

Since our first workshop in conjunction with the International Joint Conference on NLP (IJCNLP) in Chiang Mai, Thailand during Nov. 7-13, 2011 was quite successful (with 20 submissions and more than 30 participants from many countries), we planned to conduct our next workshop in conjunction with the International Conference on Computational Linguistics (COLING) being held in Mumbai, India, during Dec. 8-15, 2012. Inspired by the objectives we aimed at in the first edition of the workshop, the warm responses and feedbacks we received from the participants and attendees and the final outcome, the purpose of the 2nd edition of the Workshop on Sentiment Analysis where AI meets Psychology (SAAIP 2012) is to create a framework for presenting and discussing the challenges related to sentiment, opinion and emotion analysis in the ground of NLP. This workshop also aims to bring together the researchers in multiple disciplines such as computer science, psychology, cognitive science, social science and many more who are interested in developing next generation machines that can recognize and respond to the sentimental states of the human users. The workshop consists of a keynote talk and presentations of technical papers that have been selected after peer review from the submissions received.

The workshop starts with an invited keynote talk titled "Appraisal: a functional linguistic perspective on evaluation" by Prof. J R Martin, Department of Linguistics, University of Sydney. The talk briefly recapitulates the past two decades of research on how linguists working within the framework of systemic functional linguistics have been developing appraisal theory as a tool for analysing evaluation in discourse. The talk outlines a brief overview of the current model and then moves on to address a number of the challenges that have arisen over the years – including distinguishing inscribed from invoked attitude, determining the prosodic domain of attitude selections and the role of attitude in the negotiation of affiliation. The talk concludes by the end notes on the recent work in Maton's Legitimation Code Theory, its sociological perspective on axiologically charged constellations of meaning in particular, in relation to the above mentioned challenges.

In connection to such challenges for classifying emotions in short texts, Phillip Smith and Mark Lee present a Combinatory Categorial Grammar (CCG) based approach along with a hypothesis in which the authors adapt contextual valence shifters to infer the emotional content of a text. For classifying sentiments using machine learning approach, Basant Agarwal and Namita Mittal propose two feature selection methods, Probability Proportion Difference (PPD) and Categorical Probability Proportion Difference (CPPD) to select the relevant features. Braja Gopal Patra, Amitava Kundu, Dipankar Das and Sivaji Bandyopadhyay introduce the classification of interviews of cancer patients into several cancer diseases based on features like TF-IDF of unigram, bigram, trigram, emotion words and the SentiWordNet similarity by employing k-NN, Decision Tree and Naïve Bayes classifiers.

In the second session, Alena Neviarouskaya and Masaki Aono propose a method for automatic analysis of attitude (affect, judgment, and appreciation) in sentiment words. Rapid expansion of Web 2.0 with varieties of documents necessitates the annotation and organization of such documents in meaningful ways to expedite the search process. Thus, Akshat Bakliwal, Piyush Arora and Vasudeva Varma present a method to perform opinion mining and summarize opinions at entity level for English blogs and generate object centric opinionated summary from blogs. Yoshimi Suzuki proposes a method for classifying hotel reviews into guest's criteria, such as service, location and facilities. Such a method can be applied for review summarization.

Less attention in case of emotion recognition in speech at the linguistic level encouraged Nandini Bondale and Thippur Sreenivas to identify paralinguistic emotion markers or emotiphons for two Indian languages, Marathi and Kannada whereas K. Marimuthu and Sobha Lalitha Devi use the Reaction Time (RT) psychological index to understand how the human cognition identifies various sentiments expressed by different lexical sentiment indicators in opinion sentences. Not only cognition, music is also a universal language to convey sentiments. M. R. Velankar and H. V. Sahasrabuddhe conduct a pilot study on solo instrumental clips of bamboo flute to show that the general sentiments felt by novice Indian listeners are similar to the expected mood of specific raga of Hindustani classical music.

Xiubo Zhang and Khurshid Ahmad propose a new way of studying sentiment and capturing ontological changes in a domain specific context using affect proxies. The analysis results suggest that citations of regulatory entities show strong correlation with negative sentiments in the banking context. Finally, Zel jko Agic and Danijela Merkler conclude the session by presenting Sentiscope, a prototype system for collecting sentiment annotation and visualization of daily horoscopes from news portals written in Croatian.

This SAAIP 2012 workshop is being supported by the research project (INT/JP/JST/P-21/2009) entitled "Sentiment Analysis where AI meets Psychology", 2009 India-Japan Cooperative Programme Project

(DST-JST) jointly funded by Department of Science and Technology, Ministry of Science and Technology, Government of India and Japan Science and Technology, Government of Japan. The research project is implemented by Professor Sivaji Bandyopadhyay, Computer Science and Engineering Department, Jadavpur University, Kolkata, India and Professor Manabu Okumura, Precision and Intelligence Laboratory, Tokyo Institute of Technology, Japan.

We thank Prof. J R Martin for the keynote talk, all the members of the Program Committee for their excellent and insightful reviews, the authors who submitted contributions for the workshop and the participants for making the workshop a success. We also express our thanks to the COLING 2012 Organizing Committee and Local Organizing Committee for their support and cooperation in organizing the workshop.

Organizing Committee
2nd Workshop on Sentiment Analysis where AI meets Psychology
COLING 2012
December 15, 2012.

Organizers:

Sivaji Bandyopadhyay, Jadavpur University, Kolkata (India) (Organizing Chair)
Manabu Okumurra, Tokyo Institute of Technology, Tokyo (Japan)(Organizing Chair)
Dipankar Das, Jadavpur University (India)
Braja Gopal Patra, Jadavpur University (India)

Program Committee:

Khurshid Ahmad, Trinity College Dublin (Ireland)
Alexandra Balahur, DLSI, University of Alicante, (Spain)
Adam Bermingham, Dublin City University (Ireland)
Erik Cambria, NUS (Singapore)
Amitava Das, NTNU (Norway)
Dipankar Das, Jadavpur University (India)
Diana Inkpen, University of Ottawa (Canada)
Rada Mihalcea, University of North Texas (USA)
Alena Neviarouskaya, University of Tokyo (Japan)
Vincent Ng, University of Texas at Dallas, (USA)
Fuji Ren, University of Tokushima (Japan)
Paolo Rosso, Universidad Politécnica de Valencia (Spain)
Patrick Saint-Dizier, IRIT-CNRS (France)
Yohei Seki, Tsukuba University (Japan)
Veselin Stoyanov, Cornell University (USA)
Carlo Strapparava, Fondazione Bruno Kessler (FBK), (Italy)
Stan Szpakowicz, University of Ottawa (Canada)
Alessandro Valitutti, University of Helsinki (Finland)
Michael Zock, LIF-CNRS, Marseille (France)

Keynote Speaker:

Prof.(Dr.) J R Martin, Department of Linguistics, University of Sydney

Table of Contents

2nd Workshop on Sentiment Analysis where AI meets Psychology
Program

Saturday, 15 December 2012

09:00-09:15 Opening Remarks

09:15–10:00 *A functional linguistic perspective on evaluation*
Prof. (Dr.) J R Martin

Session 1

10:00–10:40 *A CCG-based Approach to Fine-Grained Sentiment Analysis*
Phillip Smith and Mark Lee

10:40–11:05 *Categorical Probability Proportion Difference (CPPD): A Feature Selection Method for Sentiment Classification*
Basant Agarwal and Namita Mittal

11:05–11:30 *Classification of Interviews - A Case Study on Cancer Patients*
Braja Gopal Patra, Amitava Kundu, Dipankar Das and Sivaji Bandyopadhyay

11:30–12:00 Tea break

Session 2

12:00–12:40 *Analyzing Sentiment Word Relations with Affect, Judgment, and Appreciation*
Alena Neviarouskaya and Masaki Aono

12:40–13:05 *Entity Centric Opinion Mining from Blogs*
Akshat Bakliwal, Piyush Arora and Vasudeva Varma

13:05–14:30 *Classifying Hotel Reviews into Criteria for Review Summarization*
Yoshimi Suzuki

13:30–14:30 Lunch

Session 3

14:30–15:10 *Emotiphons: Emotion Markers in Conversational Speech - Comparison across Indian Languages*
Nandini Bondale and Thippur Sreenivas

15:10–15:35 *How Human Analyse Lexical Indicators of Sentiments- A Cognitive Analysis Using Reaction-Time*
Marimuthu K and Sobha Lalitha Devi

15:35–16:00 *A Pilot Study of Hindustani Music Sentiments*
M.R. Velankar and H.V. Sahasrabuddhe

16:00–16:30 Tea break

Session 4

16:30–17:10 *Affect Proxies and Ontological Change: A finance case study*
Xiubo Zhang and Khurshid Ahmad

17:10–17:35 *Rule-Based Sentiment Analysis in Narrow Domain: Detecting Sentiment in Daily Horoscopes Using Sentiscope*
Zeljko Agic and Danijela Merkler

A Functional Linguistic Perspective on Evaluation

Prof. (Dr.) J R Martin
THE UNIVERSITY OF SYDNEY, Sydney, Australia
james.martin@sydney.edu.au

ABSTRACT

For the past two decades linguists working within the framework of systemic functional linguistics have been developing appraisal theory as a tool for analysing evaluation in discourse. In this talk I will present a brief overview of the current model and then move on to address a number of the challenges that have arisen over the years including distinguishing inscribed from invoked attitude, determining the prosodic domain of attitude selections and the role of attitude in the negotiation of affiliation. Recent work in Maton's Legitimation Code Theory, it sociological perspective on axiologically charged constellations of meaning in particular, will be introduced in relation to these challenges.

References

Macken-Horarik, M., and Martin, J. R. (Eds.). (2003). *Negotiating heteroglossia: Social perspectives on evaluation*. Mouton de Gruyter.

Martin, J. R. (2000). Beyond exchange: APPRAISAL systems in English. *Evaluation in text: Authorial stance and the construction of discourse*, *175*.

Martin, J. R., and White, P. R. (2005). *The language of evaluation*. Great Britain: Palgrave Macmillan.

http://grammatics.com/appraisal/
http://www.legitimationcodetheory.com/

A CCG-based Approach to Fine-Grained Sentiment Analysis

Phillip SMITH *Mark LEE*
School of Computer Science
University of Birmingham
Birmingham
United Kingdom, B15 2TT
P.Smith.7@cs.bham.ac.uk, M.G.Lee@cs.bham.ac.uk

ABSTRACT
In this paper, we present a Combinatory Categorial Grammar (CCG) based approach to the classification of emotion in short texts. We develop a method that makes use of the notion put forward by Ortony et al. (1988), that emotions are valenced reactions. This hypothesis sits central to our system, in which we adapt contextual valence shifters to infer the emotional content of a text. We integrate this with an augmented version of WordNet-Affect, which acts as our lexicon. Finally, we experiment with a corpus of headlines proposed in the 2007 SemEval Affective Task (Strapparava and Mihalcea, 2007), and by taking the other competing systems as a baseline, demonstrate that our approach to emotion categorisation performs favourably.

KEYWORDS: sentiment analysis, emotion classification, combinatory categorial grammar, valence shifting.

1 Introduction

Text, no matter the length, can potentially convey an emotional meaning. As the availability of digitized documents has increased over the past decade, so the ability and need to classify this data by its affective content has increased. This in turn has generated a large amount of interest in the field of Sentiment Analysis.

Typical approaches to Sentiment Analysis tend to focus on the binary classification problem of valence: whether a text has a positive or negative sentiment associated with it. The task of classifying text by its valence has been applied successfully across varying datasets, from product reviews (Blitzer et al., 2007) and online debates (Mukherjee and Liu, 2012), even spanning as far as the sentiment communicated through patient discourse (Smith and Lee, 2012). While numerous works concentrate on the binary-classification task, the next logical task in sentiment analysis, emotion classification, can sometimes be overlooked, for numerous reasons.

Emotion classification provides a more complex problem than the polarity based sentiment analysis task. While both suffer from the subtleties that the implicit nature of language holds, one of the central reasons for its complexity is that there are a greater number of categories, emotions, in which to undertake classification. Additionally, there is no fixed number of categories, as varying theories of emotion have been proposed, each detailing a slightly different subset of emotions.

This paper will provide a general approach to emotion classification, which utilises the lexical semantics of words and their combinations in order to classify a text. We will experiment with our proposed method on the SemEval 2007 Affective Task, proposed by Strapparava and Mihalcea (2007). The task offered an interesting challenge for sentiment analysis, as little data was given for training, so supervised machine learning approaches that are common to text classification on the whole, were discouraged. This therefore encouraged competing systems to consider the syntax and semantics of language when crafting their approaches to classification. The task was split into two tracks, one for traditional valence classification, and one for emotion classification. Our system experiments with the latter track.

1.1 The SemEval Data Sets and Evaluation

The corpus that was compiled for the Affective Task consisted of general news headlines obtained from websites such as Google News and CNN. Whilst a corpus of headlines is not typical for sentiment analysis, this domain was chosen for the task in hand due to the salience of the emotions that are conveyed through the use of only a few thought provoking words. It is usual for sentiment analysis to be carried out on large document sets, where documents may consist of numerous paragraphs, but in the case of this task, sentiment analysis focused on the sentence level.

The headlines provided in the corpus were annotated by six independent annotators. Six different emotions that correspond with those proposed in Ekman (1982) were used as the category labels. These six emotions were *anger*, *disgust*, *fear*, *joy*, *sadness* and *surprise*. For each emotional category, the headline was annotated on a fine-grained scale between 0 and 100, dependent upon how strongly an annotator felt that a particular emotion was expressed. For the coarse-grained evaluations of systems, each emotion was mapped to a 0/1 classification, where 0=[0,50] and 1=[50,100].

The dataset that was released consisted of two sections, a trial set and a test set. The trial set, consisted of 250 headlines, and the test set, used for evaluating the systems consisted of 1,000 annotated headlines.

1.2 Outline of Our Approach

A central part of our approach to emotion classification was the use of an appropriate lexicon. Whilst a number of lexica for sentiment analysis exist such as SentiWordNet (Esuli and Sebastiani, 2006) and AFINN (Hansen et al., 2011), as is the case with most approaches to sentiment analysis, valence is focused on, and emotions unfortunately are not considered. Therefore, in our approach to emotion classification, we use the optional lexicon of emotion bearing unigrams, WordNet-Affect, provided by the task organisers. This lexicon presents a mapping from emotional terms to the relevant emotional categories that were used to annotate the headlines in the affective task.

The WordNet-Affect dictionary alone would not suffice in a classification task from a specific genre of texts, namely headlines. WordNet-Affect contains hypernymic words associated with basic emotional concepts, but does not contain some of the more general emotion causing lexical items that are associated with headlines, such as *war*. Due to this, expansion of the lexicon with further emotion-bearing concepts was required.

Alongside the expansion of the lexicon, another occurrence in sentences needed to be taken into account: contextual valence shifters. For example, consider the sentence from the trial data set *'Budapest calm after night of violent protests'*. A basic bag-of-words approach to this may view the words (*violent, protests*) as fear, anger or sadness, whereas the only word that suggests joy is (*calm*). With a uniform scoring system in place, this headline would be incorrectly classified.

To overcome this short-coming in bag-of-words approaches to classification, sentence level valence shifters (Polanyi and Zaenen, 2006) are implemented. These influential lexical items act by altering the valence of words around them. The combination of *calm after* suggests a change in valence of the sentence, and so the phrase *night of violent protests* is shifted from a negative to positive valence.

To apply this valence shifting technology to emotion classification, we must build upon the hypothesis proposed by Ortony et al. (1988) that emotions are rooted with either a positive or negative valence, and that most words have the capability to shift valence under certain contexts. In the case of this task, we assume only joy to be associated with a positive valence, and the emotions of anger, fear, disgust, sadness and surprise stem from a negative valence. In doing this, we are able to make fine-grained emotional classifications on the headlines.

In order to implement the contextual valence shifters, a relevant parser was required that could capture adequately the functionality of valence shifting lexical entities. The Categorial Combinatory Grammar (Steedman, 2000) takes advantage of the surface syntax as an interface to the underlying compositional semantics of a language, and therefore is suitable for discovering valence shifting terms. To intergrate the CCG formalism into our system, Clark and Curran's (Clark and Curran, 2004) implementation of the parser was used.

2 Resources

To develop our system three main elements were integrated to tackle the problem of emotion classification:

- A lexicon of emotion bearing unigrams - an augmented version of WordNet-Affect
- Contextual Valence Shifters
- A Combinatory Categorial Grammar parser

These will further be described below.

2.1 WordNet-Affect

WordNet-Affect (Strapparava and Valitutti, 2004) is a lexical resource developed by extending WordNet (Fellbaum, 1998) with affective domain labels in order to produce a lexicon capable of associating affective concepts with affective words. To achieve this, WordNet-Affect (WN-A) introduces a hierarchy of affective labels whereby the included synsets are considered due to the affective concepts associated with them. This hierarchical emotional structure is modelled upon the hypernymic relations of WordNet. The affective domain labels (a-labels) consist of a number of concepts associated with affect, which include aspects such as emotion, mood, attitude and cognitive state. For the SemEval Affective Task, a subset of WN-A was released that specifically related to the six emotion categories that were used. An overview of this is given in the following table.

	Nouns	Verbs	Adjectives	Adverbs
Anger	99	64	119	35
Disgust	6	22	34	10
Fear	43	65	96	26
Joy	149	122	203	65
Sadness	64	25	169	43
Surprise	8	28	41	13

Table 1: WordNet-Affect word counts

2.2 Contextual Valence Shifters

A prevalent aspect of language is that the lexical choice of the writer is salient in conveying attitude. However, as Polanyi and Zaenen (2006) point out, the base valence of a lexical item is often modified by the polarity of its neighbouring terms, and this is something that is often overlooked in the sentiment analysis literature. For example, in the phrase *'she is not happy'*, the use of the word *not* shifts the valence of the term *happy* from a positive valence to a negative one.

However, whilst the valence may shift polarity, the same cannot be said for the emotion in the example phrase. An assumption is to uniformly shift an emotion to its presumed opposite emotion, in this case, sadness. There lies a problem with this though, as *'she is not happy'* is not equivalent to *'she is sad'*. A number of different emotions that are negatively valenced, such as anger, could be inferred from the original example sentence. Due to this, the use of the hypothesis put forward by Ortony et al. (1988) is key in determining an overall shift in emotion within a phrase or sentence.

Lexical items such as "very" and not" can be used under a variety of emotional settings, but their main role is to contribute to the strength of the resulting emotion or emotions that are conveyed within a sentence.

2.3 Combinatory Categorial Grammar

Combinatory Categorial Grammar (CCG) (Steedman, 2000) is a popular grammar formalism that builds upon combinatory logic in order to undertake efficient natural language parsing. The formalism is based upon the notion that in natural language the surface syntax acts as an interface to the underlying compositional semantics of a language.

CCGs map lexical elements of a sentence, such as nouns and adjectives, to a syntactic category. In addition to these mappings, the CCG formalism also offers a variety of combinatory rules, such as coordination and type-raising, that specify how constituent categories can be combined into larger chunks in order to provide a suitable parse for a sentence, or fragment of a sentence.

The CCG formalism provides two types of syntactic category: primitive and complex. The primitive category is recursively defined as the set of terms that include basic categories such as *V* (verb), *VP* (verb phrase), *S* (sentence) and so on. Complex categories act as functions within the grammar, and are compounds of the primitive categories. They typically take the form A/B or $A\backslash B$, where A and B are primitive categories. In this notation, the argument appears to the right on the slash, and the resulting category appears to the left of the slash. So, in the previous example, B is the argument given to the function, and A is the resulting category. The directionality of the slash indicates which side of the functor the argument must appear on. A forward slash indicates that the argument must appear to the right of the given constituent, while a backslash indicates that it must appear to the left. The following example shows how constituents combine in order to give a full parse of the sentence 'Female astronaut sets new record ':

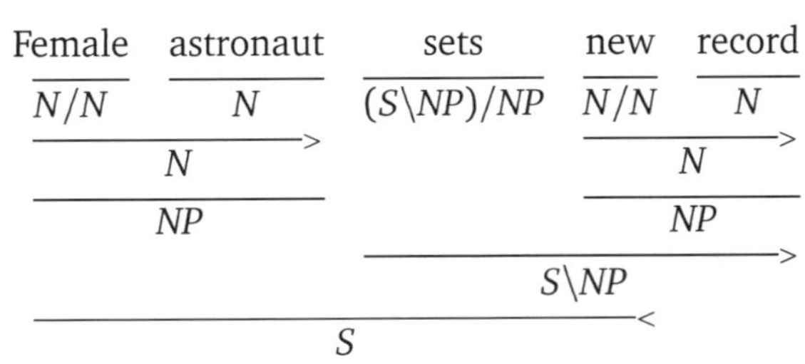

This example exhibits the *Subject-Verb-Object* construction typical of English. Here we see the verb acting as a function between the subject and object, and uses the following rule: **(S \NP)/NP**. To evaluate this, a given noun phrase should exist to the right of the function (in this case the verb) to produce the function **(S \NP)**. This then evaluates to give a sentence when a noun phrase exists to its left. If we take the phrase *'new record'*, the adjective new has the complex type **N/N**, which merely acts as a recursive function. These compositional functions enable the valence shifters described in the previous subsection to be integrated into our approach to emotion classification.

The derivation can be described with the following semantic structure:

Female	astronaut	sets	new	record
$\lambda x.female(x)$	*astronaut*	$\lambda x.\lambda y.sets(x)(y)$	$\lambda x.new(x)$	*record*
female(astronaut)			*new(record)*	
		$\lambda y.set(new(record))(y)$		
sets(new(record))(female(astronaut))				

3 The System

Our system integrates four modules to tackle the problem of emotion classification. These are: an augmented version of WN-A, which takes into account emotion bearing concepts which may have been present in headlines at the time of the task, a text-normalization unit, a CCG parser (Clark and Curran, 2004), and a lexical lookup module, dependent on the output of the contextual valence shifters, which is used to determine whether an emotional term appears in the valence-classified headline. The valence shifters that we used were adapted versions of those presented in (Simančík and Lee, 2009) and Polanyi and Zaenen (2006).

3.1 Extension of WordNet-Affect

Emotion	Associated Concepts
Anger	seize, war, bomb, sanction, attack
Disgust	porn, kidnap, desecrate, violence
Fear	Iraq, Gaza, cancer, massacre, terror, Al Qaeda
Joy	win, fun, pleasure, celebrate
Sadness	misfortune, cancel, kill, widow
Surprise	realise, discover, shock

Table 2: Some emotion concept words

The version of WordNet-Affect (WN-A) provided by the Affective Task organisers contained a set of emotion-bearing unigrams associated with the six relevant categories of the headline corpus. The terms included in this lexicon are general terms for describing an emotion, and would be useful in cross-domain classification, where the communication of emotion in text is explicit. Strapparava et al. (2006) would describe these terms in the lexicon as direct affective words. Nevertheless, the corpus involved contained headlines, which were mostly less than ten words in length, and contained few of the explicit emotion-bearing terms. Due to the implicit nature of emotional expression in the headlines, it became clear through a qualitative analysis of the training set that emotions were being associated with specific concepts and events that were the subject of the headlines.

We compiled a list of emotion bearing concepts based upon the training set and related ideas, that we believed would be pertinent within the genre of news story headlines for the period of time when the corpus was compiled, 2007. Table 2 outlines some of the lexical items that we initially compiled.

In order to augment these initial concepts we used WordNet 3.0 (Fellbaum, 1998). For the adjectives we explored and added any unique terms discovered via the *similar to* links, which helped maintain the original meaning of our set of seeds. For the nouns and verbs in the seed set we explored the hyponymic links to extend our seed set.

4 Results

	Accuracy	Precision	Recall	F1
Anger	97.82	28.57	10.53	15.38
Disgust	99.11	66.67	41.67	47.70
Fear	90.74	43.75	15.73	23.14
Joy	88.44	39.13	16.98	23.68
Sadness	90.93	57.15	32.32	41.29
Surprise	93.20	20.83	25.00	22.72
System Average	**93.35**	**42.68**	**23.70**	**28.97**
UPAR7 Comparison	89.43	27.61	5.69	8.71

Table 3: Results from our final system.

Table 3 shows the results from experimentation with our system on the test dataset, consisting of 1,000 headlines. Over the six emotional categories, our system achieved an average accuracy of 93.35%, an increase of 3.92% over the previous best system for the task, UPAR7 (Chaumartin, 2007). In the remaining coarse-grained metrics, our system also outperformed the previous best system. Our system average for precision was 42.68% , an increase of 15.07% , and our average recall value was 23.70% , also yielding a gain of 18.01% . Our resulting F1 measure delivered an increase of 20.26% .

If we consider the results on the emotion categories themselves, our system also performed favourably. In particular, the category of disgust performed well across all metrics, with a resulting accuracy of 99.11% and an F1 score of 47.70% . This can be attributed to the relatively small number of headlines labelled with the category of disgust in the test set (1.2%), which seem to describe similar news stories (such as *porn*).

Sadness also yields good results. Whilst only achieving a recall value of 32.32% , the precision sits at 57.15%, which is above the random baseline, even for a polarity based sentiment classification task. Fear and joy also share high precision values, at 43.75% and 39.13% respectively.

The classes of emotion that did not yield comparable results to the other emotional classes that were categorised during experimentation were *Anger* and *Surprise*. Anger yielded the lowest value of recall, at 10.53% and surprise the lowest precision score, at 20.83% .

5 Related Work

This section will highlight some of the systems for Sentiment Analysis that have been developed specifically for use with the headline corpus.

5.1 Systems Developed for the Emotion Classification Task

Several systems participated in the SemEval Task 14 emotion classification task. UPAR 7, a system developed by Chaumartin (2007), delivered the best performance on the emotion classification task. UPAR7 utilised an enriched version of SentiWordNet (Esuli and Sebastiani, 2006) and WordNetAffect as the base lexica for the task. Alongside these resources, the Stanford parser was used to identify salient head word structures in the headlines, and valence shifting rules based on the work of Polanyi and Zaenen (2006) were additionally implemented. The system bears a resemblance to our approach, and their final rule-based system yielded an average accuracy of 89.43% over the six-emotions of the task.

The SWAT system, developed by Katz et al. (2007), expand their training set to include an additional 1,000 headlines from the Associated Press. These were duly annotated by non-expert, untrained annotators. Roget's New Millennium Thesaurus is used to create an extensive word to emotion mapping, and this is used as SWAT's lexicon. The average accuracy achieved by the system was 88.58%, and is ranked second out of the participating systems.

The final system to take part in the emotion classification task was the UA system, developed by Kozareva et al. (2007). Their system approaches emotion classification by observing word-frequency and co-occurrence counts within online documents. They base this on the hypothesis that words which co-occur across a document-set annotated with a given emotion exhibit a high probability of expressing a particular emotion. Kozareva et al. (2007) note that they do not consider the impact of valence shifters in their work, and the shifting roles that adverbs and adjectives perform, and this may possibly have affected their overall performance. The system returns an average accuracy of 85.72% over the test set. Full results for the participating system are shown in Table 4 .

		Accuracy	Precision	Recall	F1
	Anger				
SWAT	24.51	92.10	12.00	5.00	7.06
UA	23.20	86.40	12.74	**21.6**	**16.03**
UPAR7	**32.33**	**93.60**	**16.67**	1.66	3.02
	Disgust				
SWAT	**18.55**	97.20	0.00	0.00	-
UA	16.21	**97.30**	0.00	0.00	-
UPAR7	12.85	95.30	0.00	0.00	-
	Fear				
SWAT	32.52	84.80	25.00	14.40	18.27
UA	23.15	75.30	16.23	**26.27**	**20.06**
UPAR7	**44.92**	**87.90**	**33.33**	2.54	4.72
	Joy				
SWAT	**26.11**	80.60	35.41	**9.44**	**14.91**
UA	2.35	81.80	40.00	2.22	4.21
UPAR7	22.49	**82.20**	**54.54**	6.66	11.87
	Sadness				
SWAT	38.98	87.70	32.50	11.92	17.44
UA	12.28	88.90	25.00	0.91	1.76
UPAR7	**40.98**	**89.00**	**48.97**	**22.02**	**30.38**
	Surprise				
SWAT	11.82	**89.10**	11.86	10.93	11.78
UA	7.75	84.60	**13.70**	**16.56**	**15.00**
UPAR7	**16.71**	88.60	12.12	1.25	2.27

Table 4: System results from the emotion classification task (Strapparava and Mihalcea, 2007)

5.1.1 Other systems utilising the Headline Corpus

A number of other systems developed for emotion classification post-competition also use the headline corpus as a test set for their algorithms. Mohammad (2012) created six binary classifiers for the emotions present in the headline corpus, and experimented with Logistic Regression and Support Vector Machines approaches. As supervised learning methods require sufficient data to perform adequately, the experiments deviated from the scope of the SemEval Affective Task, which was to create an emotion classification system in an unsupervised environment. The system performs well when the roles of training and test sets are swapped, but the role of training set size in overall performance should be considered. Kirange and Deshmukh (2012) also approach the task with a similar Support Vector Machines based system.

6 Discussion

In the following section we will discuss the following points in regards to our results:

- The effects of contextual valence shifters
- The inherent subjectivity associated with annotating emotions
- The role of surprise within the emotion classification spectrum

6.1 Effects of Contextual Valence Shifters

To discuss the effect that contextual valence shifters have on the task of emotion classification of headlines, it will be worth comparing our system to a basic lexical matching system, with no rules or stipulations, that uses the WordNet-Affect lexicon. The results of this are shown in Table 5.

	Accuracy	Precision	Recall	F1
Anger	97.70	25.00	10.53	14.81
Disgust	98.67	0	0	0
Fear	91.22	52.00	14.61	22.81
Joy	82.42	11.96	10.37	11.11
Sadness	89.20	26.31	5.05	8.47
Surprise	94.90	13.33	5.00	7.27

Table 5: Results from using WN-A only

If we compare the accuracy scores, improvements are only slight. However, we must remember that accuracy also takes into account false positives when calculating the overall results. If we combine this with the fact that when removing annotation scores of lower than 50 to carry out the coarse-grained evaluation of our system, then we discover that 66.5% of the headlines are classed as emotionless in the test set, despite their salience in fact being minimal. Neutral instances in sentiment classification always pose a problem, and we believe that our system deals with these appropriately, as can be seen from the gains in precision and recall over a basic lexical matching approach.

The attribute that we believe has given considerable strength to our method is the assumption that emotions are valenced. We attribute the results in general to the integration of contextual valence shifters to our system. The work of Simančík and Lee (2009) demonstrated the effectiveness of contextual valence shifters on the task in hand, and by incorporating this approach into our system, we believe that this produced the relevant increases in accuracy, precision and recall.

Interestingly enough also, UPAR 7 (Chaumartin, 2007), the previously best performing system on the emotion classification task, also utilised valence shifters in their work, which produced favourable results in comparison to the other systems. What their system may have lacked however, is the combination with a suitable grammar, such as CCG, in order to access the compositional semantics of the headlines being classified.

6.2 Comparison with Inter-Annotator Agreement

The results from our system may compare favourably to other unsupervised systems proposed for the task, but irrespective of this, our results are not exceptionally high. While this may make the system appear weak, the difficulty with recognising emotions amongst humans must be introduced, so as to give some context to the achievements of our system. Six annotators were asked to annotate the dataset with the six proposed emotions, and the results of evaluating these annotations using the Pearson correlation method are shown in Table 6.

As can be seen here, the levels of agreement do not go above 70%, and the emotion with the highest agreement is *Sadness*, at an average level of 68.19% agreement. This highlights the difficulties of annotating emotion, due to their highly subjective nature. This leads to varying levels of disagreement amongst the annotators. One particular emotion which annotators struggled to agree on is that of *surprise*.

Emotion	Agreement Score
Anger	49.55
Disgust	44.51
Fear	63.81
Joy	59.91
Sadness	68.19
Surprise	36.07

Table 6: Inter-annotator agreement scores (Strapparava and Mihalcea, 2007)

6.3 The Element of Surprise

The one emotion which both our system and others that participated in the Affective Task struggle to classify with satisfactory precision and recall is surprise. Despite outperforming other systems, with ours achieving a precision of 20.83% and recall of 25.00% , these figures are still relatively low in comparison with the other categories.

The inclusion of surprise as a category label in any corpus of emotion-bearing text is an interesting choice, and is one which may be attributed to the work of Ekman (1982). This category of surprise, however, sits in a different zone to the other emotions that are discussed throughout the task. If we refer to the work of Ortony et al. (1988) once again, they struggle to class surprise as an emotion, due to the inherently neutral nature which it can adopt. This facet is mirrored in the headlines which were annotated as containing strong elements of surprise in the headline corpus. Quite often, seemingly neutral lexical items in headlines such as *discovery* flag that a headline conveys a form of surprise. This leads to difficulties in compiling a lexicon of emotional terms related to surprise, as generally, explicit items will form the majority of this lexicon. Careful consideration of the domain, and observing token terms that are not necessarily emotion bearing, is what helped to produce the classification results for this category in our system. Due to the inherent difficulties outlined with this particular category of emotion, further corpus analysis of this phenomena is required, in particular focussing on the lexical entities associated with this emotion across domains.

Conclusions

We have developed a system for the classification of emotions held in headlines, which yields favourable classifications results in comparison with other similar systems. For the headlines in 2007 SemEval Affective Task emotion-labelled test set, our system produced higher accuracy, precision and recall scores on average than the top performing systems. The integration of the CCG parser to yield each headline's underlying compositional semantics in combination with the contextual valence shifters seems to be a very promising combination for automatic emotion annotation in headlines. To improve the scores further, an in depth understanding of the context of the domain could be integrated with the lexicon. The category of surprise also requires further study, as the available literature seems limited, yet implementing a suitable system could have positive effects on the study of automatic emotion classification. Supervised approaches to emotion classification, such as the work of Mohammad (2012) yields fruitful results, and if contextual valence shifters were integrated with this, it is believed that further increases in classification precision and recall could be produced.

Our system highlights the importance of contextual valence shifting when approaching emotion labelling. Through this work, and the successful work of others (Chaumartin, 2007; Polanyi and Zaenen, 2006) we argue that compositional semantic based valence shifters are a vital part of any system undertaking semi-supervised sentiment analysis, under the assumption that emotions are valence-rooted.

Acknowledgments

Phillip Smith is supported by the Engineering and Physical Sciences Research Council (EPSRC).

References

Blitzer, J., Dredze, M., and Pereira, F. (2007). Biographies, bollywood, boom-boxes and blenders: Domain adaptation for sentiment classification. In *Annual Meeting-Association For Computational Linguistics*, volume 45, page 440.

Chaumartin, F. (2007). UPAR7: A knowledge-based system for headline sentiment tagging. In *Proceedings of the Fourth International Workshop on Semantic Evaluations (SemEval-2007)*, pages 422–425, Prague, Czech Republic. Association for Computational Linguistics.

Clark, S. and Curran, J. R. (2004). Parsing the WSJ using CCG and Log-Linear Models. In *Proceedings of the 42nd Annual Meeting of the Association for Computational Linguistics (ACL-04)*, pages 104–111, Barcelona, Spain.

Ekman, P. (1982). *Emotion in the human face*. Cambridge University Press, New York.

Esuli, A. and Sebastiani, F. (2006). SentiWordNet: A publicly available lexical resource for opinion mining. In *Proceedings of LREC*, volume 6, pages 417–422.

Fellbaum, C. (1998). *WordNet: An Electronic Lexical Database*. MIT Press, Cambridge, MA, USA.

Hansen, L. K., Arvidsson, A., Årup Nielsen, F., Colleoni, E., and Etter, M. (2011). Good Friends, Bad News - Affect and Virality in Twitter. In *The 2011 International Workshop on Social Computing, Network, and Services (SocialComNet 2011)*.

Katz, P., Singleton, M., and Wicentowski, R. (2007). SWAT-MP:The SemEval-2007 Systems for Task 5 and Task 14. In *Proceedings of the Fourth International Workshop on Semantic Evaluations (SemEval-2007)*, pages 308–313, Prague, Czech Republic. Association for Computational Linguistics.

Kirange, D. and Deshmukh, R. (2012). Emotion Classification of News Headlines Using SVM. In *Asian Journal of Computer Science and Information Technology*, pages 104–106.

Kozareva, Z., Navarro, B., Vazquez, S., and Montoyo, A. (2007). UA-ZBSA: A Headline Emotion Classification through Web Information. In *Proceedings of the Fourth International Workshop on Semantic Evaluations (SemEval-2007)*, pages 334–337, Prague, Czech Republic. Association for Computational Linguistics.

Mohammad, S. (2012). Portable Features for Classifying Emotional Text. In *Proceedings of the 2012 Conference of the North American Chapter of the Association for Computational Linguistics: Human Language Technologies*, pages 587–591, Montréal, Canada. Association for Computational Linguistics.

Mukherjee, A. and Liu, B. (2012). Mining contentions from discussions and debates. In *Proceedings of the 18th ACM SIGKDD international conference on Knowledge discovery and data mining*, KDD '12, pages 841–849, New York, NY, USA. ACM.

Ortony, A., Clore, G. L., and Collins, A. (1988). *The Cognitive Structure of Emotions*. Cambridge University Press, New York.

Polanyi, L. and Zaenen, A. (2006). Contextual valence shifters. *Computing attitude and affect in text: Theory and applications*, pages 1–10.

Simančík, F. and Lee, M. (2009). A CCG-based system for valence shifting for sentiment analysis. *Research in Computing Science*, 41:99–108.

Smith, P. and Lee, M. (2012). Cross-discourse Development of Supervised Sentiment Analysis in the Clinical Domain. In *Proceedings of the 3rd Workshop in Computational Approaches to Subjectivity and Sentiment Analysis*, pages 79–83, Jeju, Korea. Association for Computational Linguistics.

Steedman, M. (2000). *The Syntactic Process*. The MIT Press, Cambridge, MA, USA.

Strapparava, C. and Mihalcea, R. (2007). SemEval-2007 Task 14: Affective Text. In *Proceedings of the Fourth International Workshop on Semantic Evaluations (SemEval-2007)*, pages 70–74, Prague, Czech Republic. Association for Computational Linguistics.

Strapparava, C. and Valitutti, A. (2004). WordNet-Affect: an Affective Extension of WordNet. In *Proceedings of the 4th International Conference on Language Resources and Evaluation*, Lisbon, Spain.

Strapparava, C., Valitutti, A., and Stock, O. (2006). The affective weight of lexicon. In *Proceedings of 5th International Conference on Language Resources and Evaluation (LREC 2006)*, pages 423–426, Genoa, Italy.

Categorical Probability Proportion Difference (CPPD): A Feature Selection Method for Sentiment Classification

Basant Agarwal, Namita Mittal
Department of Computer Engineering,
Malaviya National Institute of Technology, Jaipur, India
thebasant@gmail.com, nmittal@mnit.ac.in

ABSTRACT

Sentiment analysis is to extract the opinion of the user from of the text documents. Sentiment classification using machine learning methods face problem of handling huge number of unique terms in a feature vector for the classification. Thus it is required to eliminate the irrelevant and noisy terms from the feature vector. Feature selection methods reduce the feature size by selecting prominent features for better classification. In this paper, a new feature selection method namely Probability Proportion Difference (PPD) is proposed which is based on the probability of belongingness of a term to a particular class. It is capable of removing irrelevant terms from the feature vector. Further, a Categorical Probability Proportion Difference (CPPD) feature selection method is proposed based on Probability Proportion Difference (PPD) and Categorical Proportion Difference (CPD). CPPD feature selection method is able to select the features which are relevant and capable of discriminating the class. The performance of the proposed feature selection methods is compared with the CPD method and Information Gain (IG) method which has been identified as one of the best feature selection method for sentiment classification. Experimentation of proposed feature selection methods was performed on two standard datasets viz. movie review dataset and product review (i.e. book) dataset. Experimental results show that proposed CPPD feature selection method outperforms other feature selection method for sentiment classification.

KEYWORDS : Feature Selection, Sentiment Classification, Categorical Probability Proportional Difference (CPPD), Probability Proportion Difference (PPD), CPD.

1. Introduction

With the rapid growth of web technology, people now express their opinion, experience, attitude, feelings, and emotions on the web. So, it has increased the demand of processing, organizing, and analyzing the web content to know the opinion of the users (Pang B. and Lee L., 2008). An automatic sentiment text classification means to identify the sentiment orientation of the text documents i.e. positive or negative. It is important for users as well as companies to know the opinion of users, for example review for electronic products like laptop, car, movies etc. can be beneficial for users to take decision on which product to purchase and for companies to improve and market their products.
Various researchers have applied machine learning algorithms for sentiment analysis (Pang B. and Lee L., 2004; Tan S. and Zhang J., 2008; Pang B. and Lee L., 2008). One of the major problems in sentiment classification is to deal with huge number of features used for describing text documents, which produces hurdles to machine learning methods in determining the sentiment orientation of the document. Thus, it is required to select only prominent features which contribute majorly in the identification of sentiment of the document. The aim of feature selection methods is to produce the reduced feature set which is capable of determining sentiment orientation of the document by eliminating irrelevant and noisy features.
Various feature selection methods has been proposed for selecting predominating features for sentiment classification, for example Information Gain (IG), Mutual Information (MI), Chi square (CHI), Gain Ratio (GR), Document Frequency (DF) etc. (Tan S. and Zhang J., 2008; Pang B. and Lee L., 2008).

In the proposed approach, feature selection methods are used for improving the performance of the machine learning method. Initially, binary weighting scheme is used to represent the review documents, and then various feature selection methods are applied to reduce the feature set size. Further, machine learning methods are applied to the reduced and prominent feature set.

Our contribution:

1. Two new feature selection methods i.e. PPD and CPPD are proposed for sentiment classification.

2. Compared the performance of proposed feature selection methods on two different standard datasets of different domains.

The paper is organized as follows: A brief discussion of the related work is given in Section 2. Feature selection methods used for sentiment classification are discussed in Section 3. Dataset, Experimental setup and results are discussed in Section 4. Finally, conclusions and future work is described.

2. Related work

Machine learning methods have been widely applied for sentiment classification (Pang B. and Lee L., 2004; Tan S. and Zhang J., 2008; Pang B. and Lee L., 2008). Pang *et al.* 2002, applied machine learning methods viz. Support Vector Machine (SVM), Naïve Bayes (NB), and Maximum Entropy (ME) for sentiment classification on *unigram* and *bigram* features of movie review dataset. Authors found SVM to be performed best among classifiers. Authors also found that binary weighting scheme outperforms Term Frequency (TF) method for representing the text for sentiment classification. Later, a minimum cut method is proposed to eliminate objective sentences from the text (Pang B. and Lee L., 2004), which showed improved performance. Authors (Tan S. and Zhang J., 2008), experimented on five machine learning algorithms i.e. K-nearest neighbour (KNN), Centroid classifier, Winnow classifier, NB and SVM with four feature selection methods those are MI, IG, CHI, and DF for sentiment classification on Chinese documents. Authors observed that IG performs best among all the feature selection methods and SVM gives best results among machine learning algorithms.

Various feature selection methods have been proposed by various researchers for reducing the feature vector for sentiment classification for improved performance of machine learning methods (Tan S. and Zhang J., 2008; Pang B. and Lee L., 2008). Entropy Weighted Genetic Algorithm (EWGA) is proposed by combining the IG and genetic algorithm, which improved the accuracy of sentiment classification (Abbasi *et al.* 2008). Sentiment features are highlighted by increasing their weights, further authors used multiple classifiers on various feature vectors to construct the aggregated classifier (Dai *et al.* 2011). O' keefe *et al.* 2009, compared three feature selection methods for sentiment classification, which are based on Categorical Proportional Difference (CPD) and Sentiment Orientation (SO) values. Wang *et al.* 2009, proposed Fisher's discriminant ratio based feature selection method text review sentiment classification.

3. Feature selection methods

Feature selection methods select prominent features from the high dimensional feature vector by eliminating noisy and irrelevant features. Optimal feature vector improves the performance of the machine learning method in terms of both accuracy and execution time.

3.1 Probability Proportion Difference (PPD)

Probability Proportion Difference (PPD) measures the degree of belongingness or probability that a term belongs to a particular class.

Algorithm 1: Probability Proportion Difference (PPD) Feature Selection Method

Input: Document corpus (D) with labels (C) positive or negative, k (number of Optimal features to be selected)
Output: OptimalFeatureSet
Step 1 ***Preprocessing***
t ← ExtractUniqueTerms(D)
F ← TotalUniqueTerms(D)
W_p ← TotalTermsInPositiveClass(D,C)
W_n ← TotalTermsInNegativeClass(D,C)
Step 2 ***Main Feature Selection loop***
for each $t \in$ **F**
  N_{tp} =CountPositiveDocumentsInwhichTermAppears(D,t)
  N_{tn} =CountNegativeDocumentsInwhichTermAppears(D,t)
end for
for each $t \in$ **F**

$$ppd = \frac{N_{tp}}{W_p+F} - \frac{N_{tn}}{W_n+F}$$

end for
OptimalFeatureSet ← SelectTopTerm(k)

If a term has high probability of belongingness to dominantly one category/class (i.e. positive or negative) that indicates the term is important in identifying the category of unknown review. And if a term has almost equal probability of belongingness to both the categories, in that case the term is not useful in discriminating the class. PPD value of a term is calculated by computing the difference of probabilities that a term will belong to positive class or negative class. Thus, if a term has high PPD value, it indicates that the term is important for sentiment classification. Probability of belongingness of a term depends on the number of documents in which a term appears and number of unique terms appeared in that class. Algorithm for calculating PPD value of a term is given in Algorithm 1. Top k features can be selected on the basis of PPD value of the term.

3.2 Categorical Proportion Difference (CPD)

Categorical Proportional Different (CPD) value measures the degree to which a term contributes in discriminating the class (Simeon *et al.* 2008). O'Keefe *et al.* 2009, have used CPD value for feature selection method. CPD value of a term is computed by finding the ratio of the difference between the number of documents of a category in which it appears and the number of documents in which it appears of another category, to the total number of documents in which that term appears. CPD value for a feature can be calculated by using equation 1.

$$\text{cpd} = \frac{|\text{posD-negD}|}{\text{posD} + \text{negD}} \quad \text{.... (1)}$$

Here, posD is the number of positive review document in which a term appears, and negD is the number of negative review documents in which that term appear. Range of CPD value is 0 to1. If any term appears dominantly in positive or negative class, then that feature is useful for the sentiment classification, and if a term is occurring in both the categories equally then that feature is not useful for classification. If CPD value of a feature is close to 1 it means that this feature is occurring dominantly in only one category of documents. For example if "Excellent" word is occurring in 150 positive review documents and in 2 negative review documents, then value of this feature will be (150-2)/(150+2)= 0.97 , its value is near to 1 indicates that this term is useful in identifying the class of unknown document. It indicates that if a new document is having "excellent" word, there is a high chance that this document belongs to positive category. Similarly if a word occurs in same number of positive and negative documents, then CPD value will be 0, which indicates that this term is not useful for classification.

3.3 Categorical Probability Proportion Difference (CPPD)

Categorical Probability Proportion Difference (CPPD) based feature selection methods combines the merits and eliminates the demerits of both CPD and PPD methods. Benefit of CPD method is that it measures the degree of class distinguishing property of a term, which is an important attribute of a prominent feature. It can eliminate terms, which are occurring in both the classes equally and are not important for classification. It can easily eliminate the terms with high document frequency but are not important like stop words. However, PPD value of term indicates the belongingness/relatedness of a term to the classes and difference measures the class discriminating ability. It can remove the terms with less document frequency, which is not important for sentiment classification like rare terms. PPD feature selection method also considers the documents length of positive and negative reviews, since generally positive orientation documents are more in length as compared to negative class documents. So, there is a high probability that most of the feature selection method select more positive sentiment words, as compared to negative sentiment words that result in less recall. However, in the proposed CPPD method, length of documents is considered in computing the CPPD value.

Demerits of CPD feature selection method is that it can include rare term with less document frequencies but not important, which will be eliminated by PPD method. Similarly, PPD feature selection method may include term with high document frequency but not important, which will be removed by CPD method. So, by combining the merits and removing the demerits of CPD and PPD feature selection, a more reliable feature selection method is proposed for sentiment classification. CPPD feature selection method is described in algorithm2.

Algorithm 2: Categorical Probability Proportion Difference (CPPD) Feature Selection Method

Input: Document corpus (D) with labels (C) positive or negative
Output: ProminentFeatureSet
Step 1 ***Preprocessing***
$t \leftarrow$ ExtractUniqueTerms(D)
$F \leftarrow$ TotalUniqueTerms(D)
$W_p \leftarrow$ TotalTermsInPositiveClass(D,C)
$W_n \leftarrow$ TotalTermsInNegativeClass(D,C)
Step 2 ***Main Feature Selection loop***
for each $t \in \mathbf{F}$
  N_{tp} =CountPositiveDocumentsInwhichTermAppears(D,t)
  N_{tn} =CountNegativeDocumentsInwhichTermAppears(D,t)
end for
for each $t \in \mathbf{F}$
    $cpd = \frac{N_{tp}-N_{tn}}{N_{tp}+N_{tn}}$
    $ppd = \frac{N_{tp}}{W_p+F} - \frac{N_{tn}}{W_n+F}$
    if ($cpd > T1$ && $ppd > T2$)
    ProminentFeatureSet $\leftarrow$ SelectTerm(t)
end for

3.4 Information Gain (IG)

Information Gain has been identified as one of the best feature selection method for sentiment classification (Tan S. and Zhang J., 2008). Therefore, we compared proposed feature selection methods with IG. Information gain (IG) is a feature selection method, which computes importance of a feature with respect to class attribute. It is measured by the reduction in the uncertainty in classification when the value of the feature is known (Forman G. 2003). Top ranked features are selected for reducing the feature vector size in turn better classification results. IG of a term can be calculated by using equation 2 (Forman G. 2003).

$$\mathrm{IG}(t) = -\sum_{j=1}^{K} P(C_j)\log P(C_j) + P(w)\sum_{j=1}^{K} P(C_j|w)\log P(C_j|w) + P(\overline{w})\sum_{j=1}^{K} P(C_j|\overline{w})\log P(C_j|\overline{w}) \quad ..(2)$$

Here, $P(C_j)$ is the fraction of number of documents that belongs to class C_j out of total documents and $P(w)$ is fraction of documents in which term w occurs. $P(C_j|w)$ is computed as fraction of documents from class C_j that have term w and $P(C_j|\overrightarrow{W})$ is fraction of documents from class C_j that does not contain term w.

4. Experimental Setup and Result Analysis

4.1 Dataset and Experiments

One of the most popular publically available standard movie review dataset is used to test the proposed feature selection methods (Pang B., and Lee L., 2004). This standard dataset, known as Cornell Movie Review Dataset is consisting of 2000 reviews that contain 1000 positive and 1000 negative labeled reviews. In addition, product review dataset (book reviews) consisting amazon products reviews has also been used (Blitzer *et al.* 2007). This dataset contains 1000 positive and 1000 negative labeled book reviews.

Documents are initially pre-processed as follows:

(i) Negation handling, "NOT_" is added to every words occurring after the negation word (no, not, isn't, can't etc.) in the sentence. Since, a negation word inverts the sentiment of the sentence (Pang B. and Lee L., 2002).

(ii) Terms which are occurring in less than 2 documents are removed from the feature set.

The feature vector generated after pre-processing is further used for the classification. Binary weighting scheme is used for representing text since it has been proved the best method for sentiment classification (Pang B. and Lee L., 2002).

Among various machine learning algorithms Support Vector Machine (SVM) and Naïve Bayes (NB) classifiers are mostly used for sentiment classification (Pang B. and Lee L., 2002; O'Keefe *et al.* 2009; Abbasi *et al.* 2009; Pang B. and Lee L., 2008). So, in our experiments, SVM and NB are used for classifying review documents into positive or negative class. Evaluation of classification results is done by 10 folds cross validation (Kohavi R., 1995). Linear SVM and Naïve Bayes are used for all the experiments with default setting in weka machine learning tool (WEKA).

4.2 Performance measures

To evaluate the performance of sentiment classification with various feature selection methods, F-measure (given in equation 3) is used. It combines precision and recall, which are commonly used measure. Precision for a class C is the fraction of total number of documents that are correctly classified to the total number of documents that classified to the class C (sum of True Positives (TP) and False Positives (FP)).

Recall is the fraction of total number of correctly classified documents to the total number of documents that belongs to class C (sum of True Positives and False Negative (FN)).

$$F - Measure = \frac{2 * precision * recall}{(precision + recall)} \quad \ldots\ldots\ldots \quad (3)$$

4.3 Results and discussions

Some cases have been selected from movie review dataset and discussed. CPD and PPD values of some of cases have been shown in Table 1. CPD feature selection method has the drawback that less document frequent term can have very high CPD value, which is not important for classification. For example, if a term is having positive DF of 3 and negative DF of 0, then CPD value will be 1, which is maximum CPD value, even if the feature is not that important (refer case 1 of Table1). Similarly, if a term has positive DF of 1 and negative DF of 6, then CPD value comes out to be 0.714, which is quite high but the feature is not that important for classification (refer case 2 of Table1). This drawback is removed by using PPD feature selection method. Since, these types of terms have very low PPD value, so eliminated by PPD feature selection method. Also, in movie review dataset the term "poor" has low CPD value which is very important term for sentiment classification (refer case 3 of Table 1). This term will be eliminated by CPD method but would be selected by PPD method.

Similarly, cases 4, 5, 6, of Table1 for terms "Oscar", "perfect", and "bad" respectively are important for sentiment classification, which are eliminated by CPD method but included by PPD method. In contrary, few terms with high DF would have high PPD value, but not important. These terms are eliminated by CPD method. For example, In Table 1 case 7 shows PPD value high for term "because", it is eliminated by CPD method, but PPD value is high. It is due to the fact that PPD value depends on the DF and total terms in each class of the corpus. In this example, document length of positive reviews is larger as compared to length of negative reviews that is why the PPD value is high.

Cases	Positive DF	Negative DF	CPD	PPD
1	3	0	1	0.001
2	1	6	0.714	0.0016
3	57	122	0.36	0.025
4	137	62	0.375	0.024
5	201	94	0.362	0.03
6	260	515	0.329	0.099
7	461	461	0	0.011

TABLE 1. Case study of movie review dataset with different terms

Finally, by combining PPD and CPD method, a new feature selection method CPPD is proposed, which selects important features by considering the class distinguishing ability of a term and relevancy of a term based on probability with taking the size of negative and positive documents into consideration.

4.3.1 Comparison of feature selection methods

F- Measure for sentiment classification with various feature selection methods are shown in Table 2. *Unigram* feature set without any feature selection method is taken as baseline accuracy. It is observed from the experiments that all the feature selection methods improve the performance of both the classifiers (SVM and NB) as compared to baseline performance.

With CPPD feature selection method, F-measure of *unigram* feature set improves from 84.2 % to 87.5% (+3.9%) for SVM classifier and from 79.4% to 85.5 % (+7.6%) for NB classifier for movie review dataset. For book review dataset, F-measure significantly improves from 76.2% to 86% (+12.8%) for SVM classifier and from 74.5% to 80.1% (+7.5%) for NB classifier. With PPD feature selection method, F-measure improves for unigram features from 79.4% to 85.2% (+7.3%) for NB classifier and remains almost same for SVM classifier on movie review dataset.

	Movie reviews		Book reviews	
Features	SVM	NB	SVM	NB
Unigram	84.2	79.4	76.2	74.5
IG	85.8(+1.9%)	85.1(+7.1%)	84.5(+10.8%)	76.3(+2.4%)
CPD	86.2(+2.3%)	82.1(+3.4%)	82.2(+7.6%)	77.2(+3.6%)
PPD	84.1(-0.11%)	85.2(+7.3%)	84(+10.2%)	79(+6.0%)
CPPD	87.5(+3.9%)	85.5(+7.6%)	86(+12.8%)	80.1(+7.5%)

TABLE 2. F-Measure (%) for various feature selection method

4.3.2 Effect of different feature size on classification results:

F-Measure values for different feature size with various Feature Selection (FS) method for SVM classifier using movie review and book review dataset in shown in Figure 1.

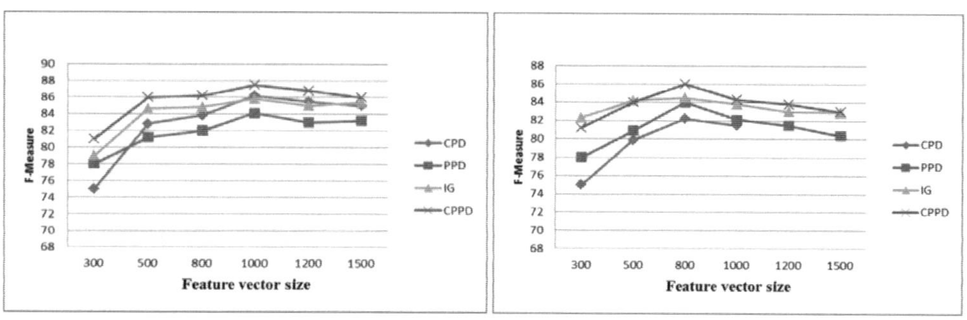

(a) (b)

FIGURE 1. (a) F-Measure (%) for various FS methods with SVM on Movie review (b) F-Measure (%) for various FS methods with SVM on Book review dataset.

It is observed from Figure 1 that CPPD method outperforms other feature selection methods. As feature size increases F-measure increases upto a certain limit, after that it varies within a small range. Best F-measure is observed for 1000 and 800 features respectively for movie review and book review dataset, which are approximately 10-15% of total unigram features.

Conclusion

Prominent feature selection for sentiment classification is very important for better classification results. In this paper, two new feature selection methods are proposed PPD and CPPD. These are compared with other FS methods namely CPD and IG. Proposed CPPD feature selection method is computationally very efficient and filters irrelevant features. It selects relevant features to the class and which can contribute in discriminating classes. The proposed schemes are evaluated on two standard datasets. Experimental results show that proposed method improves the classification performance from the baseline results very efficiently. Proposed CPPD feature selection method performs better as compared to other feature selection methods. In future, we wish to evaluate the proposed scheme on various datasets of various domains and for non-English documents.

References

Abbasi A., Chen H.C., and Salem A. (2008). "Sentiment analysis in multiple languages: Feature selection for opinion classification in web forums". *In ACM Transactions on Information Systems (TOIS),* 2008. 26(3).

Blitzer J., Dredze M., Pereira F., (2007). "Biographies, Bollywood, Boom-boxes and Blenders: Domain Adaptation for Sentiment Classification", *Proc. Assoc. Computational Linguistics. ACL Press, 2007*, pp 440-447.

Dai L., Chen H., and Li X., (2011). "Improving sentiment classification using feature highlighting and feature bagging", *In 11th IEEE International conference on Data Mining Workshops,* pp.61-66.

Forman G., (2003). "An extensive empirical study of feature selection metrics for text classification". *JMLR*, 3: pp 1289–1306.

Kohavi R., (1995). "A study of cross-validation and bootstrap for accuracy estimation and model selection", *IJCAI'95 Proceedings of the 14th international joint conference on Artificial intelligence - Vol 2*, pp1137-1143.

O'Keefe T., Koprinska I., (2009). "Feature Selection and Weighting Methods in Sentiment Analysis", In *Proceedings of the 14th Australasian Document Computing Symposium.*

Pang B., Lee L., (2008). "Opinion mining and sentiment analysis". *Foundations and Trends in Information Retrieval,* Vol. 2(1-2):pp. 1–135.

Pang B., Lee L., Vaithyanathan S., (2002). "Thumbs up? Sentiment classification using machine learning techniques", *In Proceedings of the Conference on Empirical Methods in Natural Language Processing (EMNLP),* pp. 79–86.

Pang B., Lee L., (2004). "A sentimental education: sentiment analysis using subjectivity summarization based on minimum cuts", *In Proceedings of the Association for Computational Linguistics (ACL), 2004,* pp. 271–278.

Simeon M., Hilderman R., (2008). “Categorical proportional Difference: A feature selection method for text categorization”, *In Proceedings of the 17th Australasian Data Mining Conference,* pages 201-208.

Tan S., Zhang J., (2008). "An empirical study of sentiment analysis for chinese documents”, In *Expert Systems with Applications,* vol. 34, pp. 2622-2629.

Wang S., Li D., Wei Y., Li H.,(2009). “A Feature Selection Method based on Fisher's Discriminant Ratio for Text Sentiment Classification”, *In Proceeding WISM '09 Proceedings of the International Conference on Web Information Systems and Mining,* pp 88- 97.

WEKA.Open Source Machine Learning Software Weka. http://www.cs.waikato.ac.nz/ml/weka/.

Classification of Interviews – A Case Study on Cancer Patients

Braja Gopal Patra[1] *Amitava Kundu*[1] *Dipankar Das*[2] *Sivaji Bandyopadhyay*[1]
(1) JADAVPUR UNIVERSITY, Kolkata, India
(2) NATIONAL INSTITUTE OF TECHNOLOGY, Meghalaya, India
brajagopal.cse@gmail.com, amitava.jucse@gmail.com,
dipankar.dipnil2005@gmail.com, sivaji_cse_ju@yahoo.com

ABSTRACT

With the rapid expansion of Web 2.0, a variety of documents abound online. Thus, it is important to find methods that can annotate and organize documents in meaningful ways to expedite the search process. A considerable amount of research on document classification has been conducted. However, this paper introduces the classification of interviews of cancer patients into several cancer diseases based on the features collected from the corpus. We have developed a corpus of 727 interviews collected from a web archive of medical articles. The TF-IDF features of unigram, bigram, trigram and emotion words as well as the SentiWordNet and Cosine similarity features have been used in training and testing of the classification systems. We have employed three different classifiers like *k*-NN, Decision Tree and Naïve Bayes for classifying the documents into different classes of cancer. The experimental results obtain maximum accuracy of 99.31% tested on 73 documents of the test data.

KEYWORDS: TF-IDF, document classification, cancer patients, emotion words and SentiWordNet.

1 Introduction

With the explosion of online electronic documents in recent times, document classification is becoming the necessary assistance to people in searching, organizing and collecting related documents. The task of automatic classification is a classic example of pattern recognition, where a classifier assigns labels to the test data based on the labels of the training data. Document classification is the task of assigning a document to one or more classes.

The present paper reports a task of classifying interviews of cancer patients. The primary objective is to predict the type of cancer, given a particular interview of a patient. We have developed a corpus from an open source web archive [1] of interviews conducted only for the cancer patients. The interview documents of the corpus are stored in XML format and pertaining to a total number of 17 classes of cancer. Three classifiers, namely *k*-NN, Naïve Bayes and Decision Tree were used for document classification based on TF-IDF scores and Cosine similarity. We have calculated the TF-IDF scores of unigrams, bigrams, trigrams, and emotion words. As a part of the experiment, the clustering was done by considering the similar hypernym sets of two words. We have used the scores of the word groups or WordNet clusters instead of using individual words only.

A considerable amount of research on document classification has already been conducted by different research groups such as the machine learning techniques (Sebastiani, 2002) have been adopted with great effect whereas Li and Jain, (1998) provides a brief overview of document classification. It has been observed that the Decision tree classifiers, nearest neighbor algorithms, Bayesian classifiers and support vector machines have been common choice of researchers and have produced satisfactory results. The idea is to extract the features from each document and then feed them to a machine learning algorithm (Dumais et al., 1998; Joachims, 1998). The Bag of words features such as document frequency (df) and TF-IDF features (Han et al., 2000) yield decent accuracies. Yang and Wen, (2007) achieved a maximum accuracy of 98% using TF-IDF scores of bag of words.

Enabling convenient access to scientific documents becomes difficult given the constant increase in the number of incoming documents and extensive manual labor associated with their storage, description and classification. Intelligent search capabilities are desirable so that the users may find the required information conveniently (Rak et al., 2005). This is particularly relevant for repositories of scientific medical articles due to their extensive use, large size and number and well maintained structure. The authors also report an associative classification of medical documents. Uramoto et al., (2004) developed MedTAKMI (Text Analysis and Knowledge Mining for Biomedical Documents), an application tool to facilitate knowledge discovery from very large text databases. However, the present task focuses on interview articles of the patients in cancerous conditions, as an initial step of developing a larger corpus of medical articles. It also attempts to discover semantically related word clusters from the collected interview documents. Additionally, it reports the affective statistics of the corpus and attempts to relate the frequency of emotional responses to the type of ailment of the patient. The overall aim of this research is to identify the textual clues which help in diagnosing the symptoms of the patients from their interviews. We have also incorporated the sentiment related hints so as to boost the identification of symptoms with focused perspectives.

---

[1] http://www.healthtalkonline.org/

The rest of the paper is organized in the following manner. Section 2 provides details of resource preparation. Section 3 provides an elaborative description of the features used in the task. Next, Section 4 describes the implementation of machine learning algorithms while Section 5 presents the results and analysis. Finally, conclusions and future directions are presented.

2 Resource preparation

Healthtalkonline is an award winning website that shares more than 2000 patients' experiences of over 60 health-related conditions and ailments. For our present task, we have prepared a corpus of 727 interviews of cancer patients collected from the above mentioned website. We have developed a web crawler which has been used to collect the data available on the www.healthtalkonline.org website. Once the URL of an arbitrary webpage containing a cancer related interview was supplied to the crawler, it was able to hop all other pages containing the cancer-related interviews. As such, URLs of all the webpages containing cancer interviews were spotted and thereafter, data was extracted from these pages. An initial manual examination revealed that the webpages have different formats. Thus, three kinds of patterns were observed. All unnecessary information was eliminated and the refined data was stored in XML format. A snapshot of a portion of such a XML document is shown in Figure. 1. The statistics of the corpus are given in Table 1. Out of the 727 XML documents prepared, 85% were used as training data, 5% for development and the rest 10% were used as test data. The corpus contains interviews only and is thus comprised of questions and the corresponding answers. Each line of an actual interview is either a narration/question indicative of the patient's conditions or is a response from the patient.


```
<Body>
<Situation id="1">
Aley was diagnosed with biphenotypic acute leukaemia (BAL), a mixture of myeloid and lymphoblastic leukaem
</Situation>
<QuestionAns id="1">
The day I received a call from the blood transfusion centre and a doctor said to me that I had to go and a
</QuestionAns>
<Situation id="2">
Aley broke the news to his brother in Pakistan in stages so as to prepare the family for the bombshell of
</Situation>
<QuestionAns id="2">
Then the following day I called my brother. He is older than me, three years older than me but we have got
</QuestionAns>
<Situation id="3">
Aley's treatment would definitely cause infertility but he was more concerned about curing the leukaemia t
</Situation>
<QuestionAns id="3">
Yes they did tell me and they have to store your sperm for if, because I do not have any children. I was n
</QuestionAns>
<Situation id="4">
Aley will have his white blood cells extracted and treated with UV light to counter the rash he has develo
</Situation>
```


FIGURE 1 – A Snapshot of an interview document in XML format.

Prior to feature extraction, the corpus was tokenized. Separate lists of unigrams, bigrams, trigrams, emotion words were prepared. Emotion words were identified using a SentiWordNet[2] lexicon. Some words are abundant and have little semantic content known as stop words. There were 329 stop words prepared by us manually. They were removed from the list of tokens actually utilized. Also, named entities were assumed to have little role to play in classification

[2] http://sentiwordnet.isti.cnr.it/

and hence were excluded too. Named entities were identified using the Stanford Named Entity Recognizer version 1.2.6[3]. Lists of semantically related clusters of words were prepared using hypernyms of each unigram.

Total number of words after removing stop words	421867
Total number of unique words	17627
Total number of named entity	182
Total number of Emotion words identified using SentiWordNet lexicon	5900
Total number of emotion words occurred more than three documents	3091
Total number of word classes after clubbing similar words	11466
Total number of word classes after clubbing similar words more than four documents	6287
Total number of Bigrams	201729
Total number of Bigrams occurred more than four documents	8286
Total number of Trigrams	285993
Total number of Trigrams occurred more than three documents	22082

TABLE 1 –Statistics of corpus.

3 Feature Selection

Feature selection plays an important role in machine learning framework and also in automatic document classification. Feature extraction involves simplifying the amount of resources required to describe a large set of data accurately whereas feature selection is the process of removing the irrelevant and redundant features and reducing the size of the feature set for better accuracies. The following experiments have been carried out to find out suitable features. We have used TF-IDF and Cosine Similarity feature vectors. TF-IDF of emotion words, unigrams, bigrams and trigrams have also been considered in feature vectors. The dimensionality of the feature vector space is very high. To reduce the dimensionality, semantically related unigrams were first clustered using hypernyms and then TF-IDF scores of these word groups were considered.

3.1 TF-IDF

TF-IDF is the most common weighting method which reflects the importance of each word in a document. It describes the document in a Vector space model and is used in Information Retrieval and Text Mining (Soucy and Mineau, 2005). A document is represented as the pair <t,w>, where $t=\{t_1, t_2, t_3 \ldots t_n\}$ is the set of terms and $w=\{w_1, w_2, w_3, \ldots w_n\}$ is the set of corresponding TF-IDF weights of the terms. The TF-IDF weight can be computed as follows

$$w_i = \begin{cases} \log TF(t_i, d) \times IDF(t_i) & if\ TF(t_i, d) \geq 1 \\ 0 & otherwise \end{cases}$$

Where $TF(t_i, d)$ is the frequency of the term t_i in the document d.

[3] http://nlp.stanford.edu/software/CRF-NER.shtml

$$IDF(t_i) = \log(\frac{|D|}{DF(t_i)})$$

|D| is the total number of documents and $DF(t_i)$ is the number of documents in which the term t_i is present.

3.1.1 TF-IDF of emotion words (TF-IDF$_{emo}$)

In our corpus of cancer patients' interviews, a lot of emotional responses were observed. Each interview was replete with emotion words. We have identified the emotion words from the list of unigrams using the SentiWordNet lexicon and then computed TF-IDF of these emotion words as a feature set. The aim was to find any correlation of frequency of emotion words in an interview to the severity/kind of ailment. In fact, a relatively higher number of occurrences of emotion words were observed in interviews related to certain kinds of cancer. Figure 2 illustrates the same.

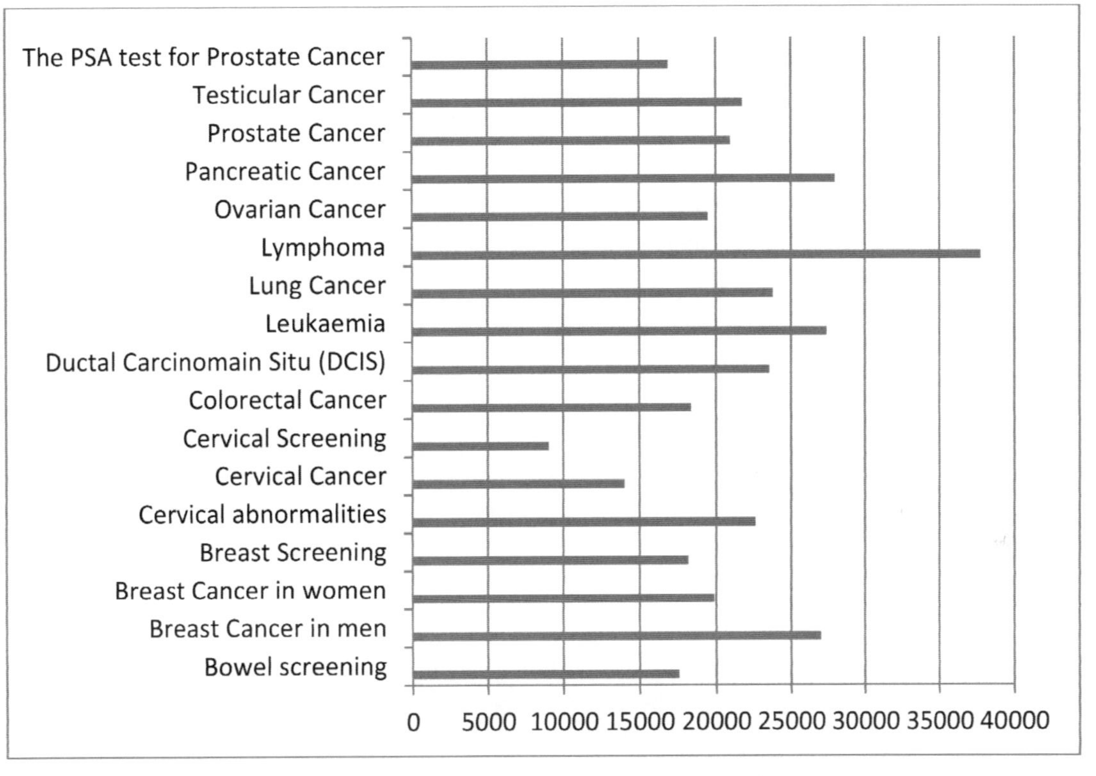

FIGURE 2 – Frequency of emotion words per cancer category

3.1.2 TF-IDF of frequent words using WordNet similarity (TF-IDF$_{wc}$)

A manual observation suggests that the words having document frequency more than four can be considered as the more useful features for our experiment. Hence, we have clubbed or clustered the similar words using hypernym relation. A hypernym is a word or phrase whose referents form a set including as a subset the referents of a subordinate term. In other words, hypernym refers to a broader meaning for a class of words. For example, 'colour' is a hypernym of 'red'. The feature vector is very large as it includes all types of features. So the feature vector is needed to be reduced to get a better result. Thus, by clustering the semantically related words, we can reduce the size of the feature vector. For the purpose, hypernyms of every unstemmed unigram were obtained by using the RitaWordnet[4] library methods.

3.1.3 TF-IDF of bigrams (TF-IDF$_B$)

We have listed the bigrams of the entire corpus. It has been found that if a bigram occurs in at least five documents, it is an effective feature in classification of documents. We have found a total of 201729 numbers of bigrams and out of these 8286 numbers of bigrams occurred in five or more documents, as shown in Table 1.

3.1.4 TF-IDF of trigrams (TF-IDF$_T$)

We have also listed the trigrams of the entire corpus. Those trigrams that occur in more than three documents have been are identified as effective features. We found a total of 285993numbers of trigrams and out of these 22082 trigrams occurred in more than three documents, as shown in Table 1.

3.2 Cosine Similarity

Cosine similarity is one of the most commonly used metrics deployed to find out the similar documents (Han et al., 2001; Dehak, 2010) from a large pool of documents. Cosine similarity is particularly effective in finding out similar documents in a high dimensional feature space. The advantage of using Cosine Similarity is that it is normalized and lies in [0,1]. Given a vocabulary V, each document d can be represented as a vector as follows:

$$\mathbf{d} = \langle tf(t_1,d), tf(t_2,d), \ldots, tf(t_{|V|},d) \rangle$$

where $t_1, t_2, .. t_{|V|}$ are the words of vocabulary V.

Given two document vectors $\mathbf{d_i}$ and $\mathbf{d_j}$, the cosine similarity between them is computed as follows

$$\cos(d_i, d_j) = \frac{\sum_{w \in V} tf(w, d_i) * tf(w, d_j)}{\sqrt{\sum_{w \in V} tf(w, d_i)^2}\sqrt{\sum_{w \in V} tf(w, d_j)^2}}$$

4 Classification of Documents

We have used three types of classifiers namely *k*-NN, Naïve Bayes and Decision Tree. The dimensionality of the feature vector space is quite high while the number of documents available in the corpus is less. Therefore, we have carried out our experiments using the above novel classifiers only instead of more complicated ones like SVM or CRF. The system architecture is given below in Figure. 3, which illustrates the steps of the task.

The corpus was first developed and cleansed during pre-processing. Thereafter, various features were extracted and the resulting data was fed to machine learning algorithms. We have used Weka 3.7.7[5] for our classification experiments. Weka is an open source data mining tool. It presents collection of machine learning algorithms for data mining tasks. 85% of the corpus was used as training data, 5% as development set and the rest 10% as test data. In order to obtain reliable accuracy, a 10-fold cross validation was performed for each classifier.

---

[4] http://rednoise.org/rita/wordnet/documentation/index.htm

[5] http://www.cs.waikato.ac.nz/ml/weka/

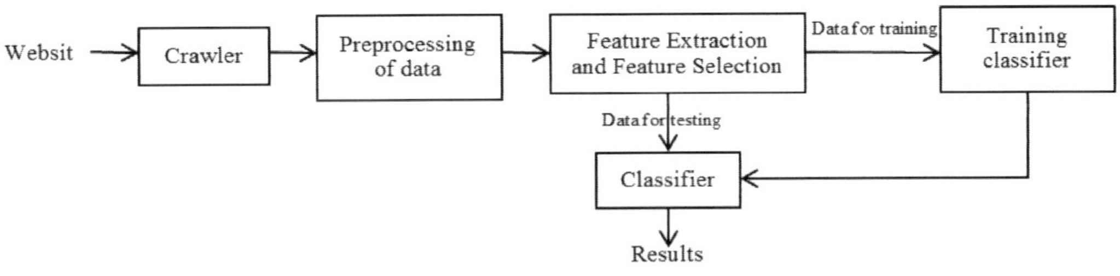

FIGURE 3 – System Architecture.

4.1 *k*-NN classifier

The documents have been represented as vectors in the TF-IDF vector space. The k-NN classifier is a learning algorithm which uses the labels of neighboring training points to decide the label of a test point. In fact, class labels of k-nearest neighbors are considered. We have used the IBk algorithm, which is an implementation of k-NN algorithm in Weka. Higher values of k are most likely to reduce the effect of outliers. However, we have used k=3 in our experiments.

4.2 Naïve Bayes classifier

Naïve Bayes is a simple probabilistic classifier based on the Bayes theorem and strong independence assumptions. The naïve Bayes model is tremendously appealing because of its robustness, elegance and simplicity. Despite being one of the oldest formal classification algorithms, it often is surprisingly effective even in its simplest forms. It is widely used for text classification purposes. We have used the multinomial Naïve Bayes classifier available in Weka tool. It is a specialized Naïve Bayes classifier for text classification.

4.3 Decision Tree classifier

We have used the J48 decision tree classifier available in the Weka tool for our purpose. J48 is actually a Java implementation of the C4.5 algorithm. C4.5 produces an initial decision tree and implements pruning in order to avoid over fitting.

5 Evaluation Results and Discussion

The interview corpus contains documents pertaining to a total of 17 classes of cancer disease. On an average, there are 40 documents per category of cancer. To obtain reliable results, we have performed a 10-fold cross validation for each of the classification experiments. The ablation study has been performed by including each of the features, separately for classification. Results obtained using bigrams, trigrams, word clusters and emotion words features have also been recorded in Table 2. The outcomes also reflect the combined effect of different features. Table 2 presents the accuracy, precision, recall and F-score of each classifier for different feature sets.

On the other hand, in a bag of words model, the Cosine similarity of documents has been considered as a feature using frequency of words only. It has been observed from the outcomes of the experiments that the Cosine similarity produces modest accuracies whereas the emotion word feature produces low accuracies compared to other TFIDF results. It is found that a total of 3091 emotion words are present on an average of three documents.

		Cosine Similarity	TF-IDF$_{emo}$	TF-IDF$_{wc}$	TF-IDF$_{B}$	TF-IDF$_{T}$	TF-IDF$_{emo}$ +TF-IDF$_{wc}$	TF-IDF$_{emo}$ +TF-IDF$_{wc}$ + TF-IDF$_{B}$	TF-IDF$_{emo}$ +TF-IDF$_{wc}$ +TF-IDF$_{B}$ +TF-IDF$_{T}$
Accuracy	*k*-NN	36.45	15.13	24.48	51.44	86.93	23.1	48.0	61.7
	Naïve Bayes	43.33	66.16	88.17	97.11	97.52	88.17	96.97	98.62
	Decision Tree	37.42	65.2	92.84	98.48	99.31	92.84	98.7	98.62
Precision	*k*-NN	38.2	28.8	53.2	67.1	91.4	47.4	56.5	77.6
	Naïve Bayes	53.5	67.5	88.9	97.2	97.6	89.0	97.1	98.7
	Decision Tree	37.4	65.9	93.0	98.5	99.3	93.0	98.7	98.6
Recall	*k*-NN	36.5	15.1	24.5	51.4	86.9	23.1	48.0	61.8
	Naïve Bayes	43.3	66.2	88.2	97.1	97.5	88.2	97.0	98.6
	Decision Tree	37.4	65.2	92.8	98.5	99.3	92.8	98.6	98.6
F-score	*k*-NN	35.6	10.7	21.9	46.0	87.5	20.2	42.1	56.3
	Naïve Bayes	40.7	66.0	88.2	97.1	97.5	88.2	97.0	98.6
	Decision Tree	37.3	65.3	92.8	98.5	99.3	92.8	98.6	98.6

TABLE 2 –Result of the experiments (in %).

It is observed that by considering the TF-IDF of word clusters, we achieved moderate accuracies and especially the bigram features produce satisfactory results. It has also been observed that the bigrams that occur in at least five documents are most informative and produce best results. The accuracies fall when bigrams occurring in more than five documents are considered, seemingly because of the reduced number of features. The trigram features have been found to be most informative feature and produce best accuracies. We have considered only those trigrams that occur in at least three documents. Another experiment has been conducted using the combined features of emotion words and word clusters. In this case, the accuracies produced are comparatively lower than that produced by trigram features. When bigram features are combined with former two features, accuracies have been improved. It has to be mentioned that further improvement in accuracies were also observed after adding the trigram features. The k-NN classifier produced low accuracies overall and J48 decision tree produces best accuracies overall.

Conclusion and future work

In this work, we have presented a task of classifying cancer patients' interviews into different types of cancer. We have performed our experiments on a corpus of 727 interview documents extracted from the healthtalkonline website. As a part of our future work, we intend to expand our corpus and include articles related to all other ailments available on the website as well. The features in the experiments have produced decent results. Maximum accuracy of 99.31% has been obtained using trigram features. Having observed abundant occurrences of emotion words in our corpus, we are planning to use our corpus for further affective analysis. Thus, our aim is to extract the patient's responses separately. In the present work, a bag of words model has been used whereas the identification of more informative features and dimensionality reduction remains another objective.

Acknowledgments

The work reported in this paper is supported by a grant from the India-Japan Cooperative Programme (DST-JST) 2009 Research project entitled "Sentiment Analysis where AI meets Psychology" funded by Department of Science and Technology (DST), Government of India.

References

Danisman, T. and Alpkocak, A. (2008). Feeler: Emotion classification of text using vector space model. In *AISB 2008 Convention Communication, Interaction and Social Intelligence*, Vol. 2, pages 53-59.

Dehak, N., Dehak, R., Glass, J., Reynolds, D. and Kenny, P. (2010). Cosine similarity scoring without score normalization techniques. In *Proceedings of Odyssey Speaker and Language Recognition Workshop*.

Dumais, S., Platt, J., Heckerman, D. and Sahami, M. (1998). Inductive learning algorithms and representations for text categorization. In *Proceedings of the seventh international conference on Information and knowledge management*, pages 148-155. ACM.

Han, E. H. and Karypis, G. (2000). Centroid-based document classification: Analysis and experimental results. *Principles of Data Mining and Knowledge Discovery*, pages116-123.

Joachims, T. (1998). Text categorization with support vector machines: Learning with many relevant features. *Machine learning: ECML-98*, pages 137-142.

Lan, M., Tan, C. L., Su, J. and Lu, Y. (2009). Supervised and traditional term weighting methods for automatic text categorization. *Pattern Analysis and Machine Intelligence, IEEE Transactions on*, *31*(4): 721-735.

Li, Y. H. and Jain, A. K. (1998). Classification of text documents. *The Computer Journal*, *41*(8): 537-546.

Quan, X., Wenyin, L. and Qiu, B. (2011). Term weighting schemes for question categorization. *Pattern Analysis and Machine Intelligence, IEEE Transactions on*, *33*(5): 1009-1021.

Rak, R., Kurgan, L. and Reformat, M. (2005). Multi-label associative classification of medical documents from medline. In *Proceedings of Fourth International Conference on Machine Learning and Applications,* pages 177-186. IEEE.

Sebastiani, F. (2002). Machine learning in automated text categorization. *ACM computing surveys (CSUR)*, *34*(1): 1-47.

Shum, S., Dehak, N., Dehak, R. and Glass, J. (2010). Unsupervised speaker adaptation based on the cosine similarity for text-independent speaker verification. In *Proc. Odyssey*.

Soucy, P. and Mineau, G. W. (2005, July). Beyond TFIDF weighting for text categorization in the vector space model. In *International Joint Conference on Artificial Intelligence*, Vol. 19, pages 1130-1135. Lawrence Erlbaum Associates Ltd.

Tasci, S. and Gungor, T. (2008). An evaluation of existing and new feature selection metrics in text categorization. In *Proceedings of 23rd International Symposium on Computer and Information Sciences, ISCIS'08*, pages 1-6. IEEE.

Uramoto, N., Matsuzawa, H., Nagano, T., Murakami, A., Takeuchi, H., and Takeda, K. (2004). A text-mining system for knowledge discovery from biomedical documents. *IBM Systems Journal*, *43*(3): 516-533.

Wen, C. Y. J. (2007). Text Categorization Based on a Similarity Approach. In *Proceedings of International Conference on Intelligent System and Knowledge Engineering*, Chengdu, China.

Xu, H., and Li, C. (2007). A Novel term weighting scheme for automated text Categorization. In *Proceedings of Seventh International Conference on Intelligent Systems Design and Applications, ISDA 2007*, pages 759-764. IEEE.

Analyzing Sentiment Word Relations with Affect, Judgment, and Appreciation

Alena NEVIAROUSKAYA   *Masaki AONO*
TOYOHASHI UNIVERSITY OF TECHNOLOGY, 1-1 Hibarigaoka, Tempaku-cho, Toyohashi, Japan
alena@kde.cs.tut.ac.jp, aono@kde.cs.tut.ac.jp

ABSTRACT

In this work, we propose a method for automatic analysis of attitude (affect, judgment, and appreciation) in sentiment words. The first stage of the proposed method is an automatic separation of unambiguous affective and judgmental adjectives from miscellaneous that express appreciation or different attitudes depending on context. In our experiments with machine learning algorithms we employed three feature sets based on Pointwise Mutual Information, word-pattern co-occurrence, and minimal path length. The next stage of the proposed method is to estimate the potentials of miscellaneous adjectives to convey affect, judgment, and appreciation. Based on the sentences automatically collected for each adjective, the algorithm analyses the context of phrases that contain sentiment word by considering morphological tags, high-level concepts, and named entities, and then makes decision about contextual attitude labels. Finally, the appraisal potentials of a word are calculated based on the number of sentences related to each type of attitude.

KEYWORDS : Appraisal potentials, Attitude lexicon, Minimal path length, Pointwise Mutual Information, Sentiment lexicon, Word-pattern co-occurrence.

1 Introduction and related work

'Attitudinal meanings tend to spread out and colour a phase of discourse as speakers and writers take up a stance oriented to affect, judgment or appreciation.' Martin and White (2005: 43)

Rapid growth of online media and sources of different genres (blogs, product or service reviews, social networks etc.) has prompted the emergence and development of a sentiment analysis field aimed at automatic analysis of people's preferences, emotions, and attitudes communicated through written language. A variety of lexical resources has been created to support recognition and interpretation of different kinds of subjective phenomena: subjective (Wilson, Wiebe, & Hoffmann, 2005), polarity (Esuli & Sebastiani, 2006; Hatzivassiloglou & McKeown, 1997; Neviarouskaya, Prendinger, & Ishizuka, 2011), affective (De Albornoz, Plaza, & Gervás, 2012; Strapparava & Valitutti, 2004), and appraisal (Argamon, Bloom, Esuli, & Sebastiani, 2007) lexicons.

The subjectivity lexicon developed by Wilson et al. (2005) is comprised by over 8000 subjectivity clues annotated by type (strongly subjective / weakly subjective) and prior polarity (positive/negative/both/neutral). Hatzivassiloglou and McKeown (1997) created a list of 1336 adjectives manually labeled as either positive or negative. Esuli and Sebastiani (2006) developed a SentiWordNet lexicon based on WordNet (Miller, 1990) synsets comprised from synonymous terms. Three numerical scores characterizing to what degree the terms included in a synset are objective, positive, and negative, were automatically determined based on the proportion of eight ternary classifiers that assigned the corresponding label to the synsets of adjectives, adverbs, nouns, and verbs by quantitatively analysing the glosses associated with them. Neviarouskaya et al. (2011) developed a SentiFul lexicon using the core of sentiment lexicon and automatically expanding it through direct synonymy and antonymy relations, hyponymy relations, and manipulations with morphological structure of words (derivation and compounding). Aimed at introducing the hierarchy of affective domain labels, Strapparava and Valitutti (2004) manually created WordNet-Affect, a lexicon of affective concepts. An affective lexicon SentiSense (De Albornoz et al., 2012) that contains concept-level emotional annotations has been developed semi-automatically by considering semantic relations between synsets in WordNet. The appraisal lexicon (Argamon et al., 2007) developed by applying supervised learning to WordNet glosses contains adjectives and adverbs annotated by attitude type and force.

Methods for extracting and annotating sentiment-related terms include: machine learning approaches examining the conjunction relations between adjectives (Hatzivassiloglou & McKeown, 1997); clustering adjectives according to distributional similarity based on a small amount of annotated seed words (Wiebe, 2000); pattern-bootstrapping algorithms to extract nouns (Riloff, Wiebe, & Wilson, 2003); consideration of web-based mutual information in ranking the subjective adjectives (Baroni & Vegnaduzzo, 2004); bootstrapping algorithm employing a small set of seed subjective terms and an online dictionary, plus filtering the candidates based on a similarity measure (Banea, Mihalcea, & Wiebe, 2008); methods employing WordNet structure relations (Andreevskaia & Bergler, 2006; Kamps & Marx, 2002; Kim & Hovy, 2004; Takamura, Inui, & Okumura, 2005); and sentiment tagging based on morphological structure of words (Ku, Huang, & Chen, 2009; Moilanen & Pulman, 2008; Neviarouskaya et al., 2011). To assign subjectivity labels to word senses, methods relying on distributional similarity (Wiebe & Mihalcea, 2006) and on semi-supervised minimum cut algorithm (Su & Markert, 2009) have been proposed.

The goal of our research is to develop a method for automatic analysis of attitude expressed by sentiment words. Such method will support analytical applications relying on recognition of fine-grained context-dependent attitudes conveyed in text. According to the Appraisal Theory (Martin & White, 2005), there are three high-level attitude types: affect (a personal emotional state, feeling, or reaction), judgment (an ethical appraisal of person's character, behaviour, skills etc.), and appreciation (an aesthetic evaluation of semiotic and natural phenomena, events, objects etc.). We distinguish sentiment-related adjectives expressing unambiguous attitude type (e.g., *happy* conveys affect, *fainthearted* – judgment, and *tasty* – appreciation) and ambiguous attitude type that depends on context (e.g., *useless* expresses affect in the context of *my useless attempts*, judgment in case of *his useless skills*, and appreciation in the phrase *useless information*).

In the first stage of the proposed method, unambiguous affective and judgmental adjectives are automatically separated from miscellaneous adjectives expressing unambiguous appreciation or different attitudes depending on context. The classification is based on a machine learning algorithm employing three feature sets based on Pointwise Mutual Information (PMI), word-pattern co-occurrence, and minimal path length. An early attempt to determine the potentials of an adjective to express affect, judgment or appreciation in evaluative discourse was made by Taboada and Grieve (2004), who calculated the PMI with the pronoun-copular pairs '*I was (affect)*', '*He was (judgement)*', and '*It was (appreciation)*'. However, affect-conveying adjectives (e.g., '*depressed*') may equally well occur not only with first person pronouns, but also with third person pronouns, thus describing emotional states experienced by oneself or by other person. Our PMI features are inspired by the approach from (Taboada & Grieve, 2004). However, as distinct from their method, we calculate the strength of the association between attitude-conveying adjectives and patterns, in which they most probably occur (the example patterns for affect and judgment are '*feel XX*' and '*XX personality*', respectively). The next stage of the proposed method is to estimate the potentials of miscellaneous adjectives to convey affect, judgment, and appreciation. Based on the sentences automatically collected for each adjective, the algorithm analyses the context of phrases that contain sentiment word and makes decision about contextual attitude labels. Finally, the appraisal potentials of a word are calculated based on the number of sentences related to each type of attitude.

The remainder of the paper is structured as follows: In Section 2, we describe the method for separation of unambiguous affective and judgmental adjectives from miscellaneous. The algorithm for estimation of the potentials of miscellaneous adjectives to express affect, judgment, and appreciation is detailed in Section 3. In next section, we conclude the paper.

2 Method for separation of unambiguous affective and judgmental adjectives from miscellaneous

2.1 Data set

For the evaluation of the proposed methodology, we have extracted 1500 attitude-annotated adjectives from the AttitudeFul database (Neviarouskaya, 2011). These adjectives are annotated by at least one of 13 labels: nine for affect (AFF), two for positive and negative judgment (JUD), and two for positive and negative appreciation (APP). As we are interested in separating unambiguous affective (e.g., *joyful*) and judgmental (e.g., *egoistic*) adjectives from miscellaneous (MISC, e.g., *good*) that express appreciation or different attitudes depending on context (for example, *good feeling* expresses positive affect, *good parent* is positive judgment, and *good book* is positive appreciation), we have considered the following top-level labels: AFF, JUD, and MISC (namely, APP and combinations AFF-APP, AFF-JUD, JUD-APP, and AFF-JUD-APP).

The distribution of classes is as follows: AFF – 510 (34.0%), JUD – 414 (27.6%), and MISC – 576 (38.4%) adjectives. The examples are listed in Table 1.

Class	Adjectives
AFF	Euphoric, disheartened, frightened, infuriated, impressed
JUD	Altruistic, brave, diligent, high-principled, tenderhearted, despotic, egoistic, ill-famed, unkind
MISC	APP: comfortable, tasty, poorly-adapted AFF-APP: healthy, devastated AFF-JUD: enthusiastic, jealous JUD-APP: adorable, cheap, nonproductive AFF-JUD-APP: balanced, calm, genuine, unfriendly, worthless

TABLE 1 – Examples of adjectives from the data set.

2.2 Feature sets

In our experiments we employed the following feature sets that are further described in details:

1. Pointwise Mutual Information (PMI) based.
2. Word-pattern co-occurrence (WPC) based.
3. Minimal path length (MPL), or proximity, based.

The complete feature set is comprised of 88 features. These features were automatically defined for each adjective from the attitude-annotated data set in order to conduct experiments with cross-validation process.

2.2.1 Pointwise Mutual Information (PMI) based feature set

The Pointwise Mutual Information had been used by researchers to calculate the strength of the semantic association between words (Church & Hanks, 1989), to determine the semantic orientation (positive or negative) of words (Turney & Littman, 2002), and to measure the strength of the association between attitude-conveying adjectives and pronoun-copular pairs, such as '*I was*', '*he was*', and '*it was*' (Taboada & Grieve, 2004). In defining PMI features we partially follow the approach from (Taboada & Grieve, 2004). However, as distinct from their method, we calculate the strength of the association between attitude-conveying adjectives and patterns, in which they most probably occur.

The Pointwise Mutual Information is calculated based on the following equation:

$$PMI(word, pattern) = \log_2 \frac{hits(word \ \ in \ a \ pattern \ )}{hits(word \ ) \times hits(pattern \ )}, \quad (1)$$

where *word* stands for one of the adjectives; *pattern* – one of the patterns for affect or judgment; and *hits* – number of hits in the search engine.

Based on the definitions from the Appraisal theory (Martin & White, 2005), we defined the patterns as indicators of affect and judgment (10 and 20 patterns, respectively). They are given in Table 2.

Affect patterns	Judgment patterns	
feel XX (e.g., *feel happy*)	XX character	XX is a character
XX emotion	XX personality	XX is a personality
XX is an emotion (e.g., *[being] happy is an emotion*)	XX trait	XX is a trait
XX as an emotion	XX behavior	XX is a behavior
XX feeling	XX behaviour	XX is a behaviour
XX is a feeling	XX skill	XX is a skill
XX as a feeling	XX skills	admire XX
XX mood	criticise XX	criticize XX
XX is a mood	praise XX	condemn XX
XX as a mood	to sanction XX	to esteem XX

TABLE 2 – Patterns for affect and judgment adjectives.

The schematic representation of the algorithm for PMI calculation is shown in Fig. 1. As a search engine, we selected BING (*http://www.bing.com/*). In our work, each BING query is submitted through BING search API (*http://www.bing.com/toolbox/bingdeveloper/*) using the following structure ensuring retrieval of exact phrases in web documents written in English:

http://api.search.live.net/xml.aspx?Appid=[application_id]*&sources=web&query=inbody:*["word_or_phrase"]*language:en.*

The total number of the returned query results (that is the number of hits) is then retrieved from the downloaded XML file.

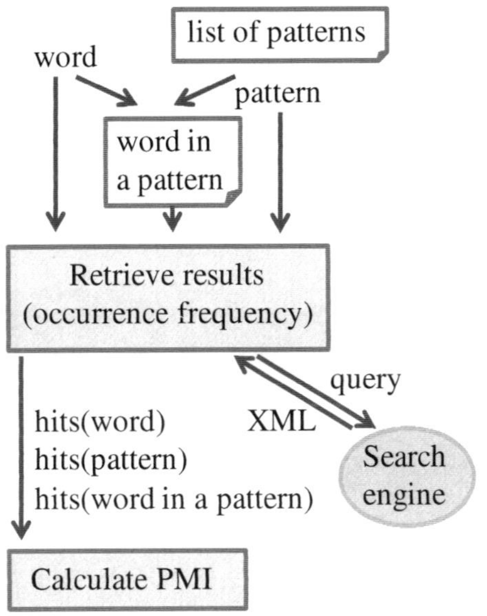

FIGURE 1 – Working flow of the PMI calculation algorithm.

There are four groups of PMI based features employed in our experiments:

1. *PMI*: PMI of an adjective with each affect pattern and each judgment pattern (in total, 30 features).
2. *maxPMI*: maximum PMI with affect patterns and maximum PMI with judgment patterns (2 features).
3. *avgPMI*: average PMI with affect patterns and average PMI with judgment patterns (2 features).
4. *%undefPMI*: percent of "undefined" PMI with affect patterns and percent of "undefined" PMI with judgment patterns (2 features). PMI with a particular pattern is "undefined" in case the search engine returns 0 for number of hits of a word in this pattern (i.e., PMI equals negative infinity).

2.2.2 Word-pattern co-occurrence (WPC) based feature set

In addition to PMI based features, we considered the following four co-occurrence based features (*max%rate*):

1. maximum percent rate of *hits(word in a pattern)* to *hits(pattern)* among affect patterns.
2. maximum percent rate of *hits(word in a pattern)* to *hits(pattern)* among judgment patterns.
3. maximum percent rate of *hits(word in a pattern)* to *hits(word)* among affect patterns.
4. maximum percent rate of *hits(word in a pattern)* to *hits(word)* among judgment patterns.

2.2.3 Minimal path length (MPL) based feature set

To establish the relatedness of a given adjective with affect or judgment, we decided to employ features based on estimation of proximity between two adjectives through synonymy relation in WordNet (Miller, 1990).

We adopted the following definitions of MPL from (Kamps & Marx, 2002):

Two words w_0 and w_n are n-related if there exists an (n+1)-long sequence of words $<w_0,w_1,...,w_n>$ such that for each i from 0 to n-1 the two words w_i and w_{i+1} are in the same SYNSET.

Let MPL be a partial function such that $MPL(w_i,w_j) = n$ if n is the smallest number such that w_i and w_j are n-related.

For the exploration of WordNet relations, we employed Java API for WordNet Searching (JAWS) publicly available at *http://lyle.smu.edu/~tspell/jaws*. Automatically analysing synonymy relations in WordNet, we estimate the shortest synonymy paths from a given adjective to each word from the representative lists of affect and judgment adjectives using Equation (2). These representative lists were created manually and include 25 affect adjectives (e.g., *angry*, *afraid*, *happy*, *downhearted*, *surprised*, and others) and 20 judgment adjectives (e.g., *clever*, *well-mannered*, *cynical*, *dishonorable*, etc.).

$$MPL(w_i, w_j) = \min\ (N)\ , \tag{2}$$

where w_i stands for one of the adjectives; w_j – one of the adjectives from representative word lists for affect and judgment; and N – set of path lengths $\{n_0,n_1,...,n_k\}$, where n_k is the number of direct-synonymy links in a synonymous sequence k between words w_i and w_j.

To make the task of analysing large synonymous network in WordNet feasible, we established the maximum limit for MPL, as the relatedness between non-direct synonyms disappears quickly when the number of synonymy links grows. Therefore, if $MPL(w_i,w_j)$ is outside the range from 0 to 4, it is considered to be >4 or undefined (no synonymy path between two words).

The feature set based on MPL contains two groups of features:

1. *MPL*: MPL between an adjective and each representative affect or judgment adjective (in total, 45 features).
2. *minMPL*: minimal MPL among MPLs between an adjective and affect adjectives and minimal MPL among MPLs between an adjective and judgment adjectives (in total, 2 features).

2.3 Classification algorithms

With the aim to find the best performing machine learning algorithm classifying attitude adjectives into AFF, JUD, and MISC classes, we conducted a series of experiments with the following algorithms from WEKA software (Hall, Frank, Holmes, Pfahringer, Reutemann, & Witten, 2009):

1. J48 (Decision Trees).
2. Naive Bayes (Bayesian classifier).
3. SMO (Sequential Minimal Optimization algorithm for training a support vector classifier).

As a baseline, we considered rule-based classifier ZeroR that classifies data using the most frequent label.

2.4 Evaluation results

We performed 10-fold cross-validations on our data set in order to get reasonable estimate of the expected accuracy on unseen adjectives.

First, we evaluated the effectiveness of distinct groups of features. The results (percents of correctly classified instances) are given in Table 3.

Groups of features	**Accuracy rate (%)**			
	ZeroR	**J48**	**Naive Bayes**	**SMO**
%undefPMI	38.40	**46.56***	44.22*	45.14*
maxPMI		**49.91***	47.99*	48.42*
max%rate		**52.30*****	36.01	38.80
avgPMI		51.67*	52.39*	**53.55***
minMPL		**54.40***	54.25*	54.25*
MPL		**55.06****	44.13*	53.51**
PMI		47.68*	54.17**	**55.08****

Best results are given in bold.
* Significantly higher than the baseline.
** Significantly higher than the baseline and one of the other methods.
*** Significantly higher than the baseline and two other methods.

TABLE 3 – Classification results using distinct groups of features.

Paired t-tests with significance level of 0.05 showed that all ML algorithms (J48, Naive Bayes, and SMO) employing distinct groups of features outperformed the baseline method with statistically significant difference in accuracy rate, with the exceptional cases of Naive Bayes and SMO using *max%rate* features. As seen from the obtained results, algorithms based on the decision trees (J48) and support vectors (SMO) overall resulted in higher accuracy than Naive Bayes classifier. *PMI* and *MPL* features proved to be more effective than other features, when employed independently in SMO and J48 algorithms, respectively.

In our next experiment, to analyse the importance of different groups of features, first we evaluated the performance of the classification algorithms with *PMI* features only, then we cumulatively added other features to the algorithms. The results in terms of accuracy rate at each step of this experiment are given in Table 4 for each classification algorithm.

Features	**Accuracy rate (%)**			
	ZeroR	**J48**	**Naive Bayes**	**SMO**
PMI	38.40	47.68*	54.17**	**55.08****
PMI + maxPMI		50.54*	54.29**	**55.40****
PMI + maxPMI + avgPMI		51.17*	55.16**	**56.85****
PMI + maxPMI + avgPMI + %undefPMI		50.50*	54.37**	**57.61*****
PMI + maxPMI + avgPMI + %undefPMI + max%rate		52.74*	50.79*	**57.77*****
PMI + maxPMI + avgPMI + %undefPMI + max%rate + MPL		57.64*	54.78*	**61.88*****
PMI + maxPMI + avgPMI + %undefPMI + max%rate + MPL + minMPL		58.47*	57.15*	**61.81*****

Best results are given in bold.
* Significantly higher than the baseline.
** Significantly higher than the baseline and one of the other methods.
*** Significantly higher than the baseline and two other methods.

TABLE 4 – Classification results based on features cumulatively added to the algorithms.

The evaluation revealed that the support vector classifier SMO significantly outperformed other methods at each step of the experiment, with only statistically insignificant difference in case of comparison to Naive Bayes at first three steps. As was expected, the obtained results indicate that the classification algorithm benefits from consideration of all groups of features. The analysis of results from the best-performing algorithm (SMO) shows that adding PMI based features, such as *maxPMI*, *avgPMI*, and *%undefPMI*, to *PMI* features allows obtaining 2.53% gain in accuracy. Insignificant improvement is observed after inclusion of WPC based features (namely, *max%rate*), and this is not surprising, as these features proved to be ineffective when independently employed in SMO (i.e., there is almost no improvement over the baseline, as seen in Table 3). Statistically significant gain in accuracy is obtained after inclusion of MPL based features (namely, *MPL* and *minMPL*). It is important to note, however, that the performance of SMO classifier does not benefit from *minMPL* features, in contrast to J48 and Naive Bayes classifiers.

The detailed accuracy of SMO with full set of features by class (AFF, JUD, and MISC) in terms of precision, recall, and F-measure is given in Table 5.

Class	Detailed accuracy of SMO		
	Precision	**Recall**	**F-measure**
AFF	0.748	0.594	0.662
JUD	0.594	0.551	0.571
MISC	0.558	0.689	0.617

TABLE 5 – Detailed accuracy of SMO with full set of features.

The classifier achieved the highest level of precision in classifying adjectives related to AFF (0.748), while it was least precise in case of MISC (0.558) adjectives. F-measures indicate that it is easier for SMO algorithm to classify AFF adjectives than MISC and JUD adjectives.

The confusion matrix (Table 6) shows that AFF and JUD adjectives were predominantly incorrectly predicted as MISC adjectives, while MISC adjectives were mostly confused with JUD ones. This is due to the fact that the MISC class in the data set includes adjectives that are annotated by multiple labels (AFF-APP, AFF-JUD, JUD-APP, AFF-JUD-APP) and may express affect or judgment depending on the context. Interesting observation is that AFF and JUD adjectives were rarely confused: only 10% of AFF adjectives were incorrectly labeled as JUD, while about 6.8% of JUD adjectives were confused with AFF ones), thus demonstrating that PMI and MPL based features proposed in our work are good enough in characterizing these categories of adjectives.

Class	AFF	JUD	MISC
AFF	303	51	156
JUD	28	228	158
MISC	74	105	397

TABLE 6 – Confusion matrix.

3 Estimation of appraisal potential

The next stage of the proposed method is to estimate the potentials of MISC adjectives to express affect, judgment, and appreciation. The schematic representation of the algorithm for appraisal potential estimation is shown in Fig. 2.

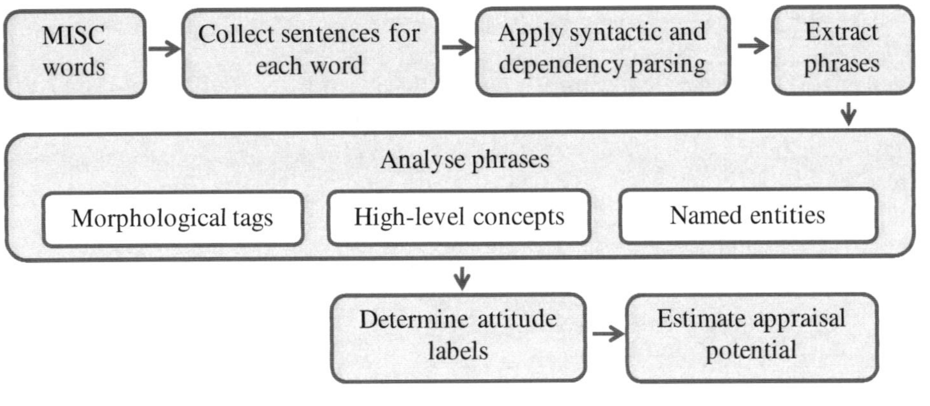

FIGURE 2 – Working flow of the algorithm for appraisal potential estimation.

The algorithm starts with the collection of sentences for each MISC word from online ABBYY Lingvo.Pro dictionary (*http://lingvopro.abbyyonline.com/en*). This dictionary allows access to unique online storage of sentences taken from real texts of different genres and language styles (classic and modern literature, web sites, technical publications, and legal documents) with the purpose to demonstrate typical use of a word. To restrict the number of example sentences extracted for each MISC adjective, the upper limit was set to 75 sentences.

Given 576 MISC adjectives, the algorithm collected 16217 sentences. About 78% of all MISC adjectives were productive, resulting in at least one example sentence. The average number of sentences per productive word is about 36. The percent distribution of productive words is as follows: low-productive adjectives (from 1 to 25 sentences) – 51.1%, including *truthful*, *inhumane*; medium-productive adjectives (from 26 to 50 sentences) – 11.3%, including *gorgeous*, *irrational*; and highly productive adjectives (from 51 to 75 sentences) – 37.6%, including *successful*, *difficult* etc. The analysis of non-productive adjectives (for example, *glamourous*, *ill-proportioned*, *uninspiring*) that did not yield any example sentence revealed that about 57% of them are hyphenated compound adjectives (for comparison, such adjectives occur only in 13% of productive ones). To collect example sentences for MISC adjectives that turned out non-productive in online ABBYY Lingvo.Pro dictionary, the algorithm may employ other online sources (for example, news, forums, blogs etc.); however, this is out of scope of this work.

Then, Connexor Machinese Syntax parser (Connexor Oy. *http://www.connexor.eu/technology/machinese/machinesesyntax/*) is applied to each sentence in order to get lemmas, syntactic relations, dependencies, syntactic and morphological information.

Using the parser output, the method then extracts phrases that include the corresponding adjective. Some examples of sentences that contain MISC adjective *beautiful* are demonstrated in Table 7.

Sentence	**Phrase**	**Annotations**	**Attitude label**
Thus all my *beautiful* feelings ended in smoke.*	my *beautiful* feelings	my [PRON PERS GEN SG1] *beautiful* feelings [N NOM PL] [*FEELING*]	AFF
She helped him to get well, and he fell madly in love with the *beautiful* young Indian and married her. **	*beautiful* young Indian	*beautiful* young Indian [N NOM SG] [*PERSON*]	JUD
'He apologizes for any inconvenience and hopes you will enjoy your stay in his *beautiful* city,' said Inigo. ***	his *beautiful* city	his [PRON PERS GEN SG3] *beautiful* city [N NOM SG] [*LOCATION*]	APP
* Youth. Tolstoy, Leo. ** The Fire From Within. Castaneda, Carlos. *** Fifth Elephant. Pratchett, Terry.			

TABLE 7 – Analysis of sentences that contain MISC adjective *beautiful*.

Three types of annotations are considered in the stage of phrase analysis (example annotations are given in Table 7):

1. morphological tags.
2. high-level concepts.
3. named entities.

Morphological tags of our particular interest that are taken from the output of Connexor Machinese Syntax parser are related to pronouns and nouns. They include N (noun), PRON (pronoun), PERS (personal), NOM (nominative), GEN (genitive), ACC (accusative), SG1/PL1 (singular/plural, first person), SG3/PL3 (singular/plural, third person), <Refl> (reflexive), <Rel> (relative), <Interr> (interrogative), and WH (wh-pronoun).

In addition to morphological tags, high-level concepts of nouns are automatically extracted from WordNet based on the analysis of bottom-up sequence of hypernymic semantic relations. The hierarchy of high-level concepts used in our approach is given in Table 8. For example, *musician* is related to high-level concept *PERSON*, *virtuosity* – to *SKILL*, and *contest* – to *EVENT*.

ENTITY	
1. ABSTRACTION	*2. ACTIVITY*
ATTRIBUTE	*3. BODY*
PERSONALITY	*4. EVENT*
SHAPE	*5. FOOD*
SKILLFULNESS	*6. LOCATION*
TRAIT	*7. OBJECT*
SELF-POSSESSION	*ARTIFACT*
COMMUNICATION	*NATURAL OBJECT*
FEELING	*8. ORGANISM*
GROUP	*ANIMAL*
ETHNIC GROUP	*HUMAN*
PEOPLE	*PERSON*
SOCIAL GROUP	*MAN*
PSYCHOLOGICAL FEATURE	*RELATIVE*
COGNITION	*9. PLANT*
ATTITUDE	*10. POSSESSION*
BELIEF, incl. *OPINION, JUDGMENT*	*11. PROCESS*
MIND	*NATURAL PHENOMENON*
SKILL	*12. STATE*
MOTIVATION, incl. *ETHICAL MOTIVE*	*13. SUBSTANCE*
QUANTITY	
RELATION	
TIME	

TABLE 8 – The hierarchy of high-level concepts.

For further annotations the algorithm employs Stanford Named Entity Recognizer (Finkel, Grenager, & Manning, 2005) to detect named entities related to *PERSON*, *ORGANIZATION*, and *LOCATION*.

Next stage is to determine attitude label for the MISC adjective depending on phrase context. The algorithm (1) analyses the morphological tags, high-level concepts, and named entities in the phrase, (2) applies rules depending on these features, and (3) makes decision about attitude label. For example, *beautiful* expresses affect in the context of *my beautiful feelings*, judgment in case of *beautiful young Indian*, and appreciation in the phrase *his beautiful city*.

The attitude label rules were developed in accordance with the definitions of affect, judgment, and appreciation given in the Appraisal Theory by (Martin & White, 2005).

- Affect is a personal emotional state, feeling, or reaction to behaviour, process, or phenomena.
- Judgment is an ethical appraisal of person's character, behaviour, skills etc. according to various normative principles.
- Appreciation is an aesthetic evaluation of semiotic and natural phenomena, events, objects etc.

The features related to AFF, JUD and APP are listed below (note that some features are common for both AFF and JUD).

- AFF: nominal head of a phrase, or subject (where adjective functions as a subject complement), or object (where adjective functions as an object complement) is

  - nominative first person pronoun (*I*, *we*), second person pronoun (*you*), or third person pronoun (*he*, *she*);
  - accusative first person pronoun (*me*, *us*), second person pronoun (*you*), or third person pronoun (*him*, *them*);
  - reflexive first person pronoun (*myself*, *ourselves*), second person pronoun (*yourself*), or third person pronoun (*herself*, *himself*);
  - relative wh-pronoun (*who*, *whoever*; *whom*, *whomever*);
  - named entity (nominative) labelled as *PERSON*;
  - one of high-level concepts: *FEELING*, *PERSON*, *MAN*, *HUMAN*, *RELATIVE*, *PEOPLE*, *ETHNIC GROUP*, or *SOCIAL GROUP*;
  - high-level concept *ACTIVITY* pre-modified by genitive first person pronoun (for example, *my useless attempts*).

  Examples of sentences, where MISC adjectives (underlined) are related to affect, include:

  It was a beneficent pause, relaxed, and filled with {<u>peaceful</u> satisfaction [N NOM SG] [*FEELING*]} *in respect of work already accomplished.* (The Magic Mountain. Mann, Thomas).

  Again was all {my [PRON PERS GEN SG1] *<u>arduous</u> labor* [N NOM SG] [*ACTIVITY*]} *gone for naught.* (The Warlord of Mars. Burroughs, Edgar Rice).

- JUD: head of a phrase, or subject (where adjective functions as a subject complement), or object (where adjective functions as an object complement) is

  - nominative first person pronoun, second person pronoun, or third person pronoun;
  - accusative first person pronoun, second person pronoun, or third person pronoun;
  - reflexive first person pronoun, second person pronoun, or third person pronoun;
  - relative wh-pronoun;
  - named entity (nominative) labelled as *PERSON* or *ORGANIZATION*;
  - one of high-level concepts: *ATTITUDE*, *BELIEF*, *MIND*, *MOTIVATION*,

PERSONALITY, SELF-POSSESSION, SKILL, SKILLFULNESS, TRAIT, PERSON, MAN, HUMAN, RELATIVE, PEOPLE, ETHNIC GROUP, SOCIAL GROUP;

- high-level concept *ACTIVITY*
  (1) pre-modified by genitive second person pronoun (*your*), genitive third person pronoun (*his*), genitive wh-pronoun (*whose*), genitive named entity labelled as *PERSON* (for example, *John's*) or *ORGANIZATION*, or genitive noun related to one of high-level concepts: *PERSON* (for example, *doctor's*), *MAN, HUMAN, RELATIVE, PEOPLE, ETHNIC GROUP, SOCIAL GROUP*, or
  (2) post-modified by phrase beginning with *of*, where prepositional complement is represented by one of named entities or high-level concepts mentioned above.

  For instance, *His acting was perfect* and *Doctor's assistance was productive* convey inscribed JUD and invoked APP, as a person is explicitly mentioned in both sentences.

Examples of sentences, where MISC adjectives (underlined) are related to judgment, include:

She has {<u>fantastic</u> organizational skills [N NOM PL] [*SKILL*]} *that have been a tremendous help in managing all the information that comes into and goes out of this office.* (Upgrading and Repairing Laptops. Mueller, Scott).

{*Russia's* [N GEN SG] [*LOCATION*] <u>*exalted*</u> *view* [N NOM SG] [*ATTITUDE*] *of itself*} *was rarely shared by the outside world.* (Diplomacy. Kissinger, Henry).

- APP: head of a phrase, or subject (where adjective functions as a subject complement), or object (where adjective functions as an object complement) is
  - named entity labelled as *LOCATION*;
  - one of high-level concepts: *ABSTRACTION, ANIMAL, ARTIFACT, ATTRIBUTE, BODY, COGNITION, COMMUNICATION, ENTITY, EVENT, FOOD, GROUP, LOCATION, NATURAL OBJECT, NATURAL PHENOMENON, OBJECT, ORGANISM, PLANT, POSSESSION, PROCESS, PSYCHOLOGICAL FEATURE, QUANTITY, RELATION, SHAPE, STATE, SUBSTANCE, TIME*;
  - high-level concept *ACTIVITY* used without explicit mention of a person (for example, *successful filtration* is a natural process (APP); the sentence *It was responsible innings* conveys inscribed APP and invoked JUD, as the person is not mentioned explicitly).

Examples of sentences, where MISC adjectives (underlined) are related to appreciation, include:

The Advisory Committee found {*the presentation* [N NOM SG] [*ACTIVITY*] *lengthy and <u>cumbersome</u>*}, *particularly in the addendum to the report.* (United Nations 2010).

He seemed to be sitting in {*a very <u>uncomfortable</u> pram* [N NOM SG] [*ARTIFACT*]}, *with some strange insects buzzing around him.* (Reaper Man. Pratchett, Terry).

After all collected sentences were labeled by attitude types, the appraisal potentials of productive MISC adjectives were estimated. The potentials of a word to express affect, judgment, and appreciation were calculated based on the number of sentences related to each type of attitude using Equations (3)-(5).

$$Affect\ Potential\ (word) = \frac{N_{aff}\ (word)}{N_{aff}\ (word) + N_{jud}\ (word) + N_{app}\ (word)} \quad (3)$$

$$Judgment\ Potential\ (word) = \frac{N_{jud}\ (word)}{N_{aff}\ (word) + N_{jud}\ (word) + N_{app}\ (word)} \quad (4)$$

$$Appreciation\ Potential\ (word) = \frac{N_{app}\ (word)}{N_{aff}\ (word) + N_{jud}\ (word) + N_{app}\ (word)}, \quad (5)$$

where *word* stands for an adjective; N_{aff}, N_{jud}, and N_{app} – number of sentences, where *word* conveys affect, judgment, and appreciation, correspondingly.

The examples of appraisal potentials calculated for adjectives are given in Table 9.

Adjective	**Affect Potential**	**Judgment Potential**	**Appreciation Potential**
appealing	0.15	0.22	0.63
awkward	0.29	0.31	0.40
bashful	0.38	0.44	0.18
consummate	0.25	0.58	0.17
excellent	0.19	0.22	0.59
genuine	0.32	0.16	0.52
jealous	0.46	0.44	0.10
loving	0.41	0.31	0.28
tasty	0.0	0.0	1.0
unsuitable	0.0	0.05	0.95
upbeat	0.5	0.33	0.17

TABLE 9 – Appraisal potentials.

Conclusions

In this paper, we proposed a novel method for analysing sentiment word relations with three attitude types, namely affect, judgment, and appreciation. We emphasized the importance of recognition of context-dependent attitudes conveyed by adjectives of ambiguous attitude type. With the aim to find the best performing machine learning algorithm classifying attitude adjectives into affect, judgment, and miscellaneous classes, we created a dataset (1500 attitude-annotated adjectives) and conducted a series of experiments with the following algorithms: Decision Trees, Naive Bayes, and Support Vector classifier. In our experiments we employed three feature sets comprising of 88 features. The evaluation revealed that the classification algorithms benefited from consideration of all groups of features, and the Support Vector classifier significantly outperformed other algorithms (with about 62% accuracy). The classifier achieved the highest level of precision in classifying adjectives related to affect (0.748), while it was least precise in case of miscellaneous (0.558) adjectives. The appraisal potentials of miscellaneous adjectives to convey affect, judgment, and appreciation were estimated based on a novel algorithm analysing contextual attitudes expressed by each word in a set of sentences.

Acknowledgments

This work was supported by a Grant-in-Aid for Scientific Research from Japan Society for the Promotion of Science (JSPS) through the program for JSPS Postdoctoral Fellowship for Foreign Researchers.

References

Andreevskaia, A. and Bergler, S. (2006). Mining WordNet for fuzzy sentiment: sentiment tag extraction from WordNet glosses. In *Eleventh Conference of the European Chapter of the Association for Computational Linguistics*, pages 209–216.

Argamon, S., Bloom, K., Esuli, A., and Sebastiani, F. (2007). Automatically determining attitude type and force for sentiment analysis. In *Third Language and Technology Conference*.

Banea, C., Mihalcea, R., and Wiebe, J. (2008). A bootstrapping method for building subjectivity lexicons for languages with scarce resources. In *International Conference on Language Resources and Evaluations (LREC 2008)*.

Baroni, M. and Vegnaduzzo, S. (2004). Identifying subjective adjectives through web-based mutual information. In *Seventh German Conference on Natural Language Processing*.

Church, K. W. and Hanks, P. (1989). Word association norms, mutual information and lexicography. In *27th Annual Conference of the Association of Computational Linguistics*, pages 76–83, New Brunswick, NJ: Association for Computational Linguistics.

De Albornoz, J. C., Plaza, L., and Gervás, P. (2012). SentiSense: An easily scalable concept-based affective lexicon for sentiment analysis. In *Eighth International Conference on Language Resources and Evaluation (LREC 2012)*.

Esuli, A. and Sebastiani, F. (2006). SentiWordNet: a publicly available lexical resource for opinion mining. In *Fifth International Conference on Language Resources and Evaluation (LREC 2006)*, pages 417–422, Genoa, Italy.

Finkel, J. R., Grenager, T., and Manning, C. (2005). Incorporating non-local information into information extraction systems by Gibbs sampling. In *43rd Annual Meeting of the Association of Computational Linguistics*, pages 363–370.

Hall, M., Frank, E., Holmes, G., Pfahringer, B., Reutemann, P., and Witten, I. H. (2009). The WEKA data mining software: An update. *SIGKDD Explorations*, 11(1).

Hatzivassiloglou, V. and McKeown, K. R. (1997). Predicting the semantic orientation of adjectives. In *35th Annual Meeting of the Association for Computational Linguistics and the 8th Conference of the European Chapter of the ACL*, pages 174–181.

Kamps, J. and Marx, M. (2002). Words with attitude. In *Belgian-Dutch Conference on Artificial Intelligence*, pages 449–450.

Kim, S.-M. and Hovy, E. (2004). Determining the sentiment of opinions. In *International Conference on Computational Linguistics (COLING 2004)*, pages 1367–1373.

Ku, L.-W., Huang, T.-H., and Chen, H.-H. (2009). Using morphological and syntactic structures for Chinese opinion analysis. In *International Conference on Empirical Methods in Natural Language Processing*, pages 1260–1269.

Martin, J. R. and White, P. R. R. (2005). *The Language of Evaluation: Appraisal in English*. Palgrave, London, UK.

Miller, G. A. (1990). WordNet: An on-line lexical database. *International Journal of Lexicography*, Special Issue, 3(4):235–312.

Moilanen, K. and Pulman, S. (2008). The good, the bad, and the unknown: morphosyllabic sentiment tagging of unseen words. In *Proceedings of the ACL-08: HLT*, pages 109–112.

Neviarouskaya, A. (2011). *Compositional Approach for Automatic Recognition of Fine-Grained Affect, Judgment, and Appreciation in Text*. PhD Dissertation, Graduate School of Information Science and Technology, University of Tokyo.

Neviarouskaya, A., Prendinger, H., and Ishizuka, M. (2011). SentiFul: A lexicon for sentiment analysis. *IEEE Transactions on Affective Computing*, 2(1):22–36.

Riloff, E., Wiebe, J., and Wilson, T. (2003). Learning subjective nouns using extraction pattern bootstrapping. In *Conference on Natural Language Learning*, pages 25–32.

Strapparava, C. and Valitutti, A. (2004). WordNet-Affect: an affective extension of WordNet. In *International Conference on Language Resources and Evaluation*, pages 1083–1086.

Su, F. and Markert, K. (2009). Subjectivity recognition on word senses via semi-supervised mincuts. In *North American Association of Computational Linguistics (NAACL 2009)*.

Taboada, M. and Grieve, J. (2004). Analyzing appraisal automatically. In *AAAI Spring Symposium on Exploring Attitude and Affect in Text*, pages 158–161.

Takamura, H., Inui, T., and Okumura, M. (2005). Extracting semantic orientation of words using spin model. In *43rd Annual Meeting of the Association of Computational Linguistics*, pages 133–140.

Turney, P. and Littman, M. (2002). Unsupervised learning of semantic orientation from a hundred-billion-word corpus. *Technical Report ERC-1094 (NRC 44929)*, National Research Council of Canada.

Wiebe, J. (2000). Learning subjective adjectives from corpora. In *17th Conference of the AAAI*.

Wiebe, J. and Mihalcea, R. (2006). Word sense and subjectivity. In *Joint Conference of the International Committee on Computational Linguistics and the Association for Computational Linguistics (COLING-ACL 2006)*.

Wilson, T., Wiebe, J., and Hoffmann, P. (2005). Recognizing contextual polarity in phrase-level sentiment analysis. In *Human Language Technology Conference and Conference on Empirical Methods in Natural Language Processing*, pages 347–354, Vancouver, Canada: Association for Computational Linguistics.

Entity Centric Opinion Mining from Blogs

Akshat Bakliwal, Piyush Arora, Vasudeva Varma
Search and Information Extraction Lab,
LTRC, International Institute of Information Technology, Hyderabad
akshat.bakliwal@research.iiit.ac.in, piyush.arora@research.iiit.ac.in,
vv@iiit.ac.in

ABSTRACT
With the growth of web 2.0, people are using it as a medium to express their opinion and thoughts. With the explosion of blogs, journal like user-generated content on the web, companies, celebrities and politicians are concerned about mining and analyzing the discussions about them or their products. In this paper, we present a method to perform opinion mining and summarize opinions at entity level for English blogs. We first identify various objects (named entities) which are talked about by the blogger, then we identify the modifiers which modify the orientation towards these objects. Finally, we generate object centric opinionated summary from blogs. We perform experiments like named entity identification, entity-modifier relationship extraction and modifier orientation estimation. Experiments and Results presented in this paper are cross verified with the judgment of human annotators.

KEYWORDS: Sentiment Analysis, Opinion Mining, English Blog, Object Identification, Opinion Summary.

1 Introduction

A Blog is a web page where an individual or group of users record opinions, information, etc. on a regular basis. Blogs are written on many diverse topics like politics, sports, travel and even products. However, the quality of the text generated from these sources is generally poor and noisy. These texts are informally written and suffer from spelling mistakes, grammatical errors, random/irrational capitalization (Dey and Haque, 2008).

Opinion Mining from blogs aims at identifying the viewpoint of the author about the objects[1]. Summarizing these expressed viewpoints can be useful for many business and organizations where they analyze the sentiment of the people on a product, or for an individual(s) who are curious to know opinions of other people. Current approaches on opinion identification divide the larger problem (document) into sub-problems (sentences) and approach each sub-problem separately. These approaches have a drawback that they cannot capture the context flow and opinion towards multiple objects within the blog.

Blog summarization task is considered as normal text summarization, without giving significance to the nature and structure of the blog. Current state of art summarization systems perform candidate sentences selection from the content and generate the summary.

In this paper[2], we present a new picture to blog opinion mining, an entity perspective blog opinion mining and summarization. Here, we identify the objects which the blogger has mentioned in the blog along with his view points on these objects. In this work, named entities are potential objects for opinion mining. We perform opinion mining for each of these objects by linking modifiers to each of these objects and deciding the orientation of these modifiers using a pre-constructed subjective lexicon. And finally, we generate two different concept summaries: an object wise opinionated summary of the document and opinionated summary of the object across the dataset.

2 Related Work

The research we propose here is a combination of Opinion Mining and Summarization. (Pang et al., 2002; Turney, 2002) started the work in the direction of document level sentiment analysis. Major work in phrase level sentiment analysis was initially performed in (Agarwal et al., 2009; Wilson, 2005). (Hu and Liu, 2004; Liu and Hu, 2004; Popescu and Etzioni, 2005) concentrated on feature level product review mining. They extracted features from product reviews and generated a feature wise opinionated summary. Blog sentiment classification is primarily performed at document and sentence level. (Ku et al., 2006) used TREC and NTCIR blogs for opinion extraction. (Chesley, 2006) performed topic and genre independent blog classification, making novel use of linguistic features. (Zhang and et al., 2007) divided the document into sentences and used Pang (Pang et al., 2002) hypothesis to decide opinion features. (He et al., 2008) proposed dictionary based statistical approach which automatically derives the evidence for subjectivity from blogs. (Melville et al., 2009) and (Draya et al., 2009) are among few other works on blog sentiment analysis.

MEAD (Radev et al., 2004) is among the first few and most widely used summarizing systems. (Arora and Ravindran, 2008) perform multi-document summarization. In (Zhou and Hovy, 2005), authors try to summarize technical chats and email discussions.

[1] In this article, we shall refer to named entity(ies) as object(s).

[2] Due to space constraints, we have eliminated some parts and discussions. Extended version of this paper is available at http://akshatbakliwal.in

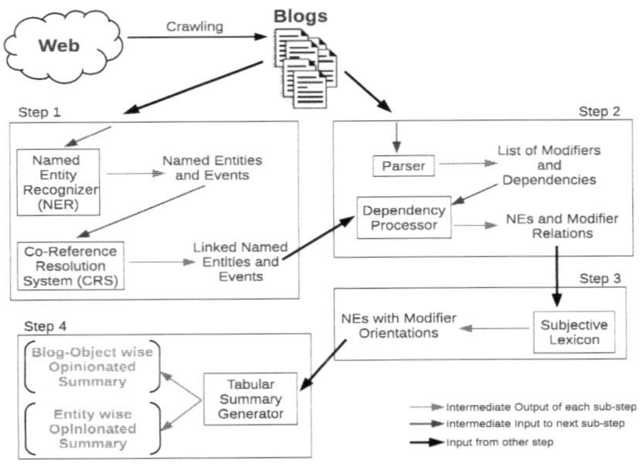

Figure 1: Algorithmic Flow of the proposed approach

Our work derives its motivation from (Hu and Liu, 2004; Liu and Hu, 2004). They identified product features and generated an opinionated summary from product reviews. In our task, the data is more formal (structured with less grammatical and spelling errors) and we generate opinionated summaries of objects (person, organizations, etc). Our summary differs from a conventional summary because we don't pick candidate sentences directly from the text, we pick only entities and opinion words towards those entities.

3 Proposed Approach

In this research, we present a new and different approach towards blog opinion analysis. Apart from the traditional approaches of classifying a blog at the sentence and document level, we describe an approach which uses the connectivity and contextual information mined using parsing. The approach proposed here depends on two lexical resources, Stanford CoreNLP[3] Tool and SentiWordNet (Baccianella et al., 2010). Stanford CoreNLP tool includes Parser, Part-of-Speech Tagger (PoS), Named Entity Recognizer (NER), Co-reference Resolution System (CRS). Our approach can be viewed as comprising of four major steps. *Figure 1* represents the architecture of the approach proposed highlighting all the sub-modules and intermediate inputs and outputs.

1. Object Identification: What is an Object? An Object is the entity the blogger is talking and expressing his views about. A blog can have multiple objects which are discussed at varied level of depths. In this step we extract the objects from the input blog. There are various techniques that can be used for performing object identification, using Named Entity Recognizer and Noun Phrase patterns (Hu and Liu, 2004; Liu and Hu, 2004).

2. Modifier Identification: What are object modifiers? An object modifier is usually an adjective, an adverb or a verb which modifies the object directly or indirectly. In this step we extract the modifiers from the blog and map them to the objects identified in Step 1. In this step, we find all the modifiers and link them to corresponding objects. In the subsequent steps we use only those modifiers which are linked to any object. We focus primarily on adjective modifier (amod), adverb modifier (advmod), nominal subject (nsubj), etc types of dependencies from Stanford parser to link modifiers to their

[3]http://nlp.stanford.edu/software/corenlp.shtml

Source	Telegraph (telegraph.co.uk)
Domain	Sports
Number of Blogs	100
Number of Unique Objects	1984
Number of Modifiers	4540

Table 1: Summary of Blog Dataset

objects. For ex. 'Ram Lal is a good boy.', for this example following are the collapsed dependencies: nn(Lal-2,Ram-1); nsubj(boy-6,Lal-2); cop(boy-6,is-3); det(boy-6,a-4); amod(boy-6,good-5). Using the nn tag 'Ram' and 'Lal' are combined a single entity [Ram Lal], amod tag maps 'good' (adjective) to 'boy' (noun) and nsubj tag maps 'boy' (noun) to 'Lal' [Ram Lal].

3. Modifier Orientation: What really is Modifier Orientation? Every adjective, adverb and verb have some implicit polarity (positive, negative or neutral) associated with them. With this polarity they modify the orientation of the objects. Once we get the objects being talked about in the blog and also have the modifiers with respect to each of these objects, the next important task is to assign subjectivity scores to these modifiers. We use SentiWordNet(Baccianella et al., 2010) to determine the polarity of each modifier.

4. Summary Generation: We generate an entity wise opinionated summary in the last step. We generate two different kinds of summaries, blog level and entity wise.

   At blog level, after assigning orientation to each of the modifier for a particular entity, we generate a tabular summary of the whole blog which has two main parts, different entities and events being talked about and opinion orientation with respect to each entity. Template of the summary is as follows: <Entity, Opinion Words, Opinion Orientation>

   In entity wise summary, we collect all the opinions expressed across all the blogs on that entity. After collecting all the opinions we generate a summary for each of the entities. Template of the summary is as follows: <Entity, Opinion Words, Opinion Orientation,Number of Blogs, List of Blog titles>

4 Dataset

We have collected 100 blogs from Telegraph[4] in sports domain. These blogs are from various categories like London Olympics, Cricket, Boxing, etc. While working on this data, we observed that blogs are usually comparison between two or more objects like “X is better than Y under some circumstances”. Hence, we have found many objects in the blog but we find very few opinion words for various entities. Refer *Table 1* for the dataset used in this research.

We decided to go with a more formal dataset because of two reasons. Firstly, there was no dataset available aprior which was annotated in the required format. Secondly, to avoid any form of biasness while collecting the dataset, we simply crawled top 100 blogs from Telegraph sports section. Although this dataset is free from most of the anomalies present in general blog data, but helps us to present the essence of our proposed approach very clearly. A few observations we made while working on blog dataset were: Much of the information present in

[4]telegraph.co.uk

the blog(s) were factual, most of the opinions expressed were either in comparison format or negatively orientated.

4.1 Evaluation Setup

In this subsection, we explain the method used for evaluating our approach. We hired three human annotators for this task and calculation of their mutual agreement is done using Cohen's Kappa measurement[5]. Validation task was divided into three basic steps

1. Object Identification: Each human annotator was asked to identify all the named entities (person, organizations, location, etc) from the text. This process is similar to step 1 of our proposed approach. *Table 2* gives the agreement of human annotators for object identification.

	Total Unique Objects Identified	Total Unique Modifiers Identified
Annotator 1	1984	3690
Annotator 2	1698	3740
Annotator 3	1820	3721
Average κ Score	**0.856**	**0.818**

Table 2: Manual agreement scores for Object and Modifier Identification

2. Modifier Identification: After step 1, they were asked to mark and decide the orientation (positive or negative) for all the modifier words (adjectives, adverbs and verbs) from the text. This step involved a good understanding of English language and word usage. This corresponds to step 2 of our approach. *Table 2* gives the agreement of human annotators for modifier identification.

3. Object-Modifier Relation: Here, they were asked to assign/link modifiers to named entities i.e. to determine the opinion of the blogger towards the objects. This step was the most tricky step as it requires a clear understanding of language construct(s). This corresponds to step 3 in our approach where we use dependency processor to handle this. Dependency Processor is a module which reads the typed dependencies retrieved from stanford parser and relates the attributes of these dependency tags with each other.

In the end, for the cases where the annotators failed to achieve an agreement, first and second authors of this paper performed the task of annotation to resolve the disagreement. *Table 3* gives the kappa (κ) statistics of human agreement for each of these tasks.

One striking observation we made was that majority of the modifiers were negatively orientated i.e. blogs are frequently written to express negative sentiments (or disagreement) about the object.

5 Experiments and Results

We divide the experiment into four steps as discussed in *Section 3* (Approach). In this section, we describe the experiment using a small running example[6] from the corpus. We illustrate the

[5]http://en.wikipedia.org/wiki/Cohen's_kappa

[6]Title: Channel 4 unveils Paralympic Games broadcast team - Clare Balding, Jon Snow leading lights

Channel 4 **today unveiled their main possee of presenters.** Clare Balding **and Jon Snow - the** **veteran** **news** anchor **(anchor) who will oversee the Opening and Closing Ceremonies - the heavy hitters in a team with plenty of broadcasting experience, plenty of sports broadcasting nous, but in some ways only a smattering of Paralympic Games experience.**

...

Snow: no one **better** in the business, and with a sensitive touch for a hard man anchor.

...

Peak time live coverage of the Games on Channel 4 will be fronted by **renowned** sports broadcaster Clare Balding and TV presenter and former Paralympic wheelchair basketball medalist Ade Adepitan.

Figure 2: Image highlights named entities in the piece of text. Words in bold highlight the modifiers and Words coloured using same colour highlight same entities.

Kappa (κ) score between annotator 'i' and annotator 'j' (κ_{ij})	
κ_{12}	**0.875**
κ_{13}	0.827
κ_{23}	0.842
Average κ Score	**0.848**

Table 3: Kappa Scores for Manual Agreement

tools we have used for each step with a small description. We also highlight the task done in each step for snippet example in *Figure 2*.

- Step 1, we identify the objects using NER (Stanford NER). We use NER over noun phrase patterns because noun phrase patterns tend to introduce more noise. There can be many noun phrases which have no named entities. And also, we have to use some method (like association rule mining) to discard non relevant noun phrases. After performing named entity identification, we then perform co-reference resolution to link all the instances of these entities together, using CRS (Stanford Co-reference Resolution). Stanford NER and Stanford CRS tools were available in Stanford CoreNLP toolkit.

  Using Stanford NER, our system discovered a total 1756 unique named entities from 1984 unique named entities tagged by human annotators. In the sample snippet shown in *Figure 2*, we have 4 named entities "Channel 4", "Clare Balding", "Jon Snow" and "Ade Adepitan".

- In Step 2, we identify adjectives, adverbs and verbs which modify the named entities identified in step 1. We link the named entities and modifiers using the dependencies (like amod, advmod, nsubj, etc) given by Stanford parser. We perform dependency association to a level of depth 2. We also discard all the modifiers which are not mapped to any named entity as they are of no use to our system later. Stanford parser and Stanford part-of-speech used in this step is also available in Stanford CoreNLP toolkit.

  Using Stanford parser and part-of-speech tagger, our system discovered 3755 correct modifiers (adjectives + adverbs + verbs). This is 82.7% of what human annotators identified (4540). For the sample snippet in *Figure 2* mappings (modifier to entity) are shown in *Table 4*.

- Using SentiWordNet, we identified the orientation of these modifiers in Step 3. We use the most common used sense of each word for scoring in order to handle multiple senses of each word. While deciding the orientation of a modifier, we perform negation handling and take in account for negative words (like not, no , never, *n't, etc.) preceding it within a window of 3 words to the left..

Modifier	Object	Parser Dependency
<>	Channel 4	<>
Veteran	Clare Balding	amod(veteran, anchor); dep(anchor, Balding)
Veteran	John Snow	amod(veteran, anchor); dep(anchor, Balding); conj_and(Balding, Snow)
Better	John Snow	advmod(better, one); dep(one, Snow)
Renowned	Clare Balding	amod(renowned, Balding)
<>	Ade Adepitan	<>

Table 4: Object to Modifier Mapping steps

Object	Modifier(s)	Orientation
Channel 4	< >	Neutral
Clare Balding	<veteran, renowned>	Positive
Jon Snow	<veteran, better>	Positive
Ade Adepitan	<medalist>	Positive

Table 5: Blog-Object Summary for the example

- In Step 4, we create a tabular summary of objects and their respective modifiers (Refer *Table 5*). This summary belongs to type 1 : Blog level summary. Using this kind of summary, we can draw a picture of user's mind and how he/she thinks about various entities. The second type of summary generated can be used to compare two different entities.

Table 6 reports the accordance of our proposed algorithm with human annotators. Opinion orientation agreement is calculated as an aggregate opinion towards an entity.

One plausible reason for decent agreement of our system with manual annotation is that, most of the external tools (Stanford CoreNLP, Parser, PoS tagger) we used in this research are trained on Wall Street Journal News wire data. Our dataset is also taken from a news website, and is written by professional content writers.

Unique objects identified by human annotators	1984
Unique objects identified by our system	1919
Correct Unique objects identified by our system	1756
Object identification coverage	**88.5%**
Total modifiers tagged by human annotators	4540
Total modifiers tagged by our system	4690
Correct Total modifiers tagged by our system	3755
Modifier identification coverage	**82.7%**
Opinion orientation agreement (aggregate)	**81.4%**

Table 6: Results of the system proposed and developed in this research

6 Discussion

In this section, we discuss some of the challenges we faced while working with the tools used in the above approaches. We try to illustrate the drawbacks of the tools with help of examples, specific for each step.

- In step 1, we proposed the use of NER. We covered $\sim$ 82.7% of the named entities tagged by human annotators. Stanford NER failed to detect multi word organization names at many places. For example "Great Britain basketball squad" in this example Stanford NER tagged "Great Britain" as a location and didn't tag basketball squad (tagged as 'Other'). But in actual, this whole should be tagged as an organization. For another example "GB Performance Director Chris Spice", in this example all the words in this phrase were tagged as an organization but here "Chris Spice" should have been tagged as person.
- In step 2, we use the parser and part-of-speech information derived using Stanford Parser and PoS tagger. These tools also produced some errors, for example in one of the blogs, "match-winning" is tagged as an adjective and in another example, "fine-innings" is tagged as an adjective.
- We use SentiWordNet to decide the polarity of each modifier in step 3. This is a general lexicon built for large purpose sentiment analysis and doesn't cover various words which are specific to sports domain. Words which are specific to sports domain like "medalist", "winner" are not present in such lexicons, and thus we need to build a domain specific lexicon.

We perform entity centric opinion mining on blogs because blogs are document like big collection of text. In blogs, context flows within sentences, across sentences and across multiple paragraphs. It is very hard to perform sentiment analysis at document and sentence level because there are multiple objects being talked about and also at varied level of depths. Calculating the overall opinion is difficult and also it will not present the correct picture. Thus, in this research, we first identify the objects (entities) and perform sentiment analysis and opinion mining across the entities. For example, *"England batted poorly, but credit to Saeed Ajmal for a quite superb performance, ending up with career-best figures of 7-55."* in this sentence, there are multiple opinions. We discuss this example in more detail in *Appendix A*.

Traditional N-Gram based approaches have following limitations: limited training data, diverse topics, context dependency and vocabulary mismatch. Problem of limited training data, context dependency (partial) and vocabulary mismatch are addressed by far using our approach. Our proposed approach is not completely hassle free. Our approach has these limitations: no prior established annotated dataset, determining modifier orientation and poor performance on complex dependency relations.

Conclusion

Blog opinion identification and summarization is an interesting task which will be very useful for businesses to analyze users' opinion at a fine grained feature level, for governments to understand the fall backs in the policies introduced. We described a method to generate opinionated summary of various entities within the blog and also across the corpus in an automated manner. We achieved $\sim$86% agreement in object identification, $\sim$83% accordance in modifier orientation and $\sim$81% agreement in opinion orientation identification.

References

Agarwal, A., Biadsy, F., and Mckeown, K. R. (2009). Contextual phrase-level polarity analysis using lexical affect scoring and syntactic n-grams. In *Proceedings of the 12th Conference of the European Chapter of the ACL (EACL)*.

Arora, R. and Ravindran, B. (2008). Latent dirichlet allocation based multi-document summarization. In *Proceedings of the second workshop on Analytics for noisy unstructured text data*, AND '08.

Baccianella, S., Esuli, A., and Sebastiani, F. (2010). Sentiwordnet 3.0: An enhanced lexical resource for sentiment analysis and opinion mining. In *Proceedings of the Seventh conference on International Language Resources and Evaluation (LREC'10)*.

Chesley, P. (2006). Using verbs and adjectives to automatically classify blog sentiment. In *In Proceedings of AAAI-CAAW-06, the Spring Symposia on Computational Approaches*.

Dey, L. and Haque, S. K. M. (2008). Opinion mining from noisy text data. In *Proceedings of the second workshop on Analytics for noisy unstructured text data*, AND '08.

Draya, G., Plantié, M., Harb, A., Poncelet, P., Roche, M., and Trousset, F. (2009). Opinion mining from blogs. In *International Journal of Computer Information Systems and Industrial Management Applications (IJCISIM)*.

He, B., Macdonald, C., He, J., and Ounis, I. (2008). An effective statistical approach to blog post opinion retrieval. In *Proceedings of the 17th ACM conference on Information and knowledge management*, CIKM '08.

Hu, M. and Liu, B. (2004). Mining and summarizing customer reviews. In *Proceedings of the tenth ACM SIGKDD international conference on Knowledge discovery and data mining (KDD'04)*.

Ku, L.-W., Liang, Y.-T., and Chen, H.-H. (2006). Opinion extraction, summarization and tracking in news and blog corpora. In *AAAI Spring Symposium: Computational Approaches to Analyzing Weblogs*.

Liu, B. and Hu, M. (2004). Mining opinion features in customer reviews. In *Proceedings of American Associatoin for Artifical Intelligence (AAAI'04)*.

Melville, P., Gryc, W., and Lawrence, R. D. (2009). Sentiment analysis of blogs by combining lexical knowledge with text classification. In *Proceedings of the 15th ACM SIGKDD international conference on Knowledge discovery and data mining*, KDD '09.

Pang, B., Lee, L., and Vaithyanathan, S. (2002). Thumbs up? sentiment classification using machine learning techniques. In *Proceedings of the 2002 Conference on Empirical Methods in Natural Language Processing (EMNLP)*.

Popescu, A.-M. and Etzioni, O. (2005). Extracting product features and opinions from reviews. In *Proceedings of the conference on Human Language Technology and Empirical Methods in Natural Language Processing (HLT-EMNLP'05)*.

Radev, D., Allison, T., Blair-Goldensohn, S., and Blitzer (2004). Mead- a platform for multidocument multilingual text summarization. In *Conference on Language Resources and Evaluation (LREC)*.

Turney, P. D. (2002). Thumbs up or thumbs down?: semantic orientation applied to unsupervised classification of reviews. In *Proceedings of the 40th Annual Meeting on Association for Computational Linguistics*.

Wilson, T. (2005). Recognizing contextual polarity in phrase-level sentiment analysis. In *In Proceedings of HLT-EMNLP*.

Zhang, W. and et al. (2007). Opinion retrieval from blogs. In *In Proceedings of the sixteenth ACM conference on Conference on information and knowledge management (2007)*.

Zhou, L. and Hovy, E. (2005). Fine-grained clustering for summarizing chat logs. In *Proceedings of the Workshop on Beyond Threaded Conversation, held at the Computer-Human Interaction conference (CHI2005)*.

Appendix A

Word	Lemma	PoS	NER
England	England	NNP	Location
batted	bat	VBD	O
poorly	poorly	RB	O
,	,	,	O
but	but	CC	O
credit	credit	NN	O
to	to	TO	O
Saeed	Saeed	NNP	Person
Ajmal	Ajmal	NNP	Person
for	for	IN	O
a	a	DT	O
quite	quite	RB	O
superb	superb	JJ	O
performance	performance	NN	O
,	,	,	O
ending	end	VBG	O
up	up	RP	O
with	with	IN	O
career-best	career-best	JJ	O
figures	figure	NNS	O
of	of	IN	O
7-55	7-55	CD	Number
.	.	.	O

Table 7: Results of Stanford CoreNLP on the sample sentence

Here, we provide the output of Stanford CoreNLP for the sentence *"England batted poorly, but credit to Saeed Ajmal for a quite superb performance, ending up with career-best figures of 7-55."* in *Table 7*. *Figure 3* shows the output of Part-of-speech tagger. *Figure 4* shows the output of

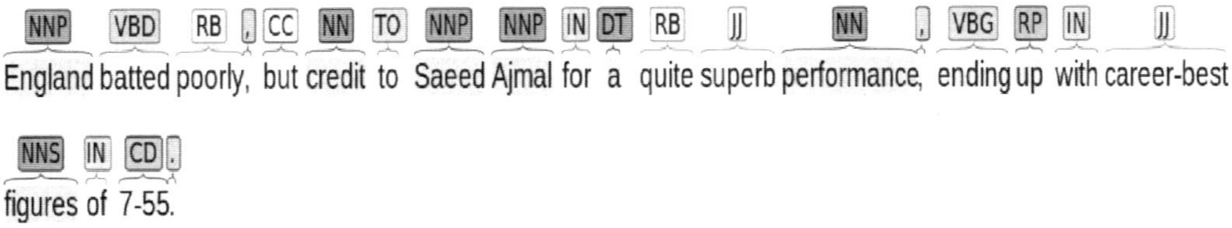

Figure 3: Figure shows the output of Part-of-speech tagger for the sample sentence

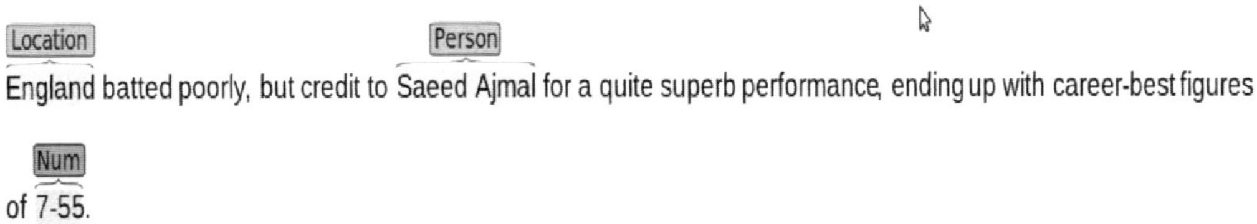

Figure 4: Figure shows the output of Named Entity Recognizer for the sample sentence

named entity recognizer and in *Figure 5* we show the collapsed dependencies for the sample sentence. We have taken *Figure 3, 4, 5* from here[7]. If we consider the sentence as a whole unit, we cannot predict concretely whether it is positive, negative or neutral sentence but if we look entity wise, we can construct a clear representation for it. We have mainly 2 entities "England" and "Saeed Ajmal" which are referred in this sentence. The entity wise analysis will yield us the following results:

– England: batted poorly. (Negative). Negative sentiment is imparted by adverb "poor". "poor" is connected with "batted" using an adverb modifier (advmod) tag and "batted" is connected to "England" by nominal subject (nsubj) tag. *Figure 5* highlight all these connections.

– Saeed Ajmal: quite superb performance. (Positive). Positive adjective ("superb") is linked to "performance" using adjective modifier (amod) relation and "performance" is linked to "Ajmal" via preposition for (prep_for). In this way, we get the positive sentiment towards *Saeed Ajmal*. This entity wise representation provides us with a clear picture of the sentence and overcomes the limitation of sentence level sentiment classification.

In this example, we can also see that "England" is identified incorrectly by Stanford NER. Here "England" should have been identified as an organization (England Cricket Team) rather than as location.

[7]http://nlp.stanford.edu:8080/corenlp/

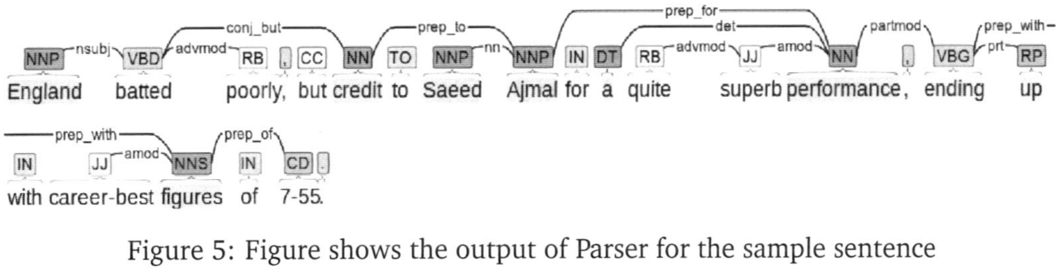

Figure 5: Figure shows the output of Parser for the sample sentence

Classifying Hotel Reviews into Criteria for Review Summarization

Yoshimi SUZUKI
University of Yamanashi, 4-3-11 Takeda, Kofu, Yamanashi, JAPAN
`ysuzuki@yamanashi.ac.jp`

ABSTRACT
Recently, we can refer to user reviews in the shopping or hotel reservation sites. However, with the exponential growth of information of the Internet, it is becoming increasingly difficult for a user to read and understand all the materials from a large-scale reviews. In this paper, we propose a method for classifying hotel reviews written in Japanese into criteria, *e.g.*, location and facilities. Our system firstly extracts words which represent criteria from hotel reviews. The extracted words are classified into 12 criteria classes. Then, for each hotel, each sentence of the guest reviews is classified into criterion classes by using two different types of Naive Bayes classifiers. We performed experiments for estimating accuracy of classifying hotel review into 12 criteria. The results showed the effectiveness of our method and indicated that it can be used for review summarization by guest's criteria.

KEYWORDS: hotel reviews, text segmentation, guest's criteria.

1 Introduction

Recently, we can refer to user reviews in the shopping or hotel reservation sites. Since the user's criteria are included in the user review compared with the information offering by a contractor, there is a possibility that many information which is not included in a contractor's explanation but included in the reviews. These customer/guest reviews often include various information about products/hotels which are different from commercial information provided by sellers/hotel owners, as customers/guests have pointed out with their own criteria, *e.g.*, service may be very important to one guest such as business traveler whereas another guest is more interested in good value for selecting a hotel for his/her vacation. Using Consumer Generated Media (CGM) such as hotel reviews, we can obtain different perspective from commercial information. However, there are at least six problems to deal with user reviews:

1. There are a large amount of reviews for each product/hotel.
2. Each review is short.
3. Each review includes overlapping contents.
4. Some reviews include wrong information.
5. The terms are not unified.
6. There are various sentiment expressions.

Moreover, there are many compound sentences in hotel reviews. Similarly, there are two or three criteria in a compound sentence. In order to deal with six problems mentioned in the above, we propose a method for classifying hotel reviews into criteria, such as service, location and facilities. We extracted criterion words and classified sentences of reviews into criteria. We can detect important sentences for review summarization by using the results of criteria extraction.

2 Related work

Our study is to extract list of reviewers' criteria and their sentiment expression. The approach is classified into sentiment analysis and text segmentation. Sentiment analysis is one of the challenging tasks of Natural Language Processing. It has been widely studied and many techniques (Beineke et al., 2004; Yi and Niblack, 2005; Hu and Liu, 2004), have been proposed. Wei et al. proposed HL-SOT (Hierarchical Learning process with a defined Sentiment Ontology Tree) approach (Wei and Gulla, 2010) to label a product's attributes and their associated sentiments in product reviews. Text segmentation has also been well studied. Utiyama and Isahara proposed a statistical method for domain-independent text segmentation (Utiyama and Isahara, 2001). Hirao et al. attempted the use of lexical cohesion and word importance (Hirao et al., 2000). They employed two different methods for text segmentation. One is based on lexical cohesion considering co-occurrences of words, and another is base on the changes of the importance of each sentence in a document.

3 System overview

Figure 1 illustrates an overview of our system. The system consists of two modules, namely "Classification of criterion words" and "Classification of review sentences into criteria". Hotel reviews written in Japanese are classified into criteria by the system.

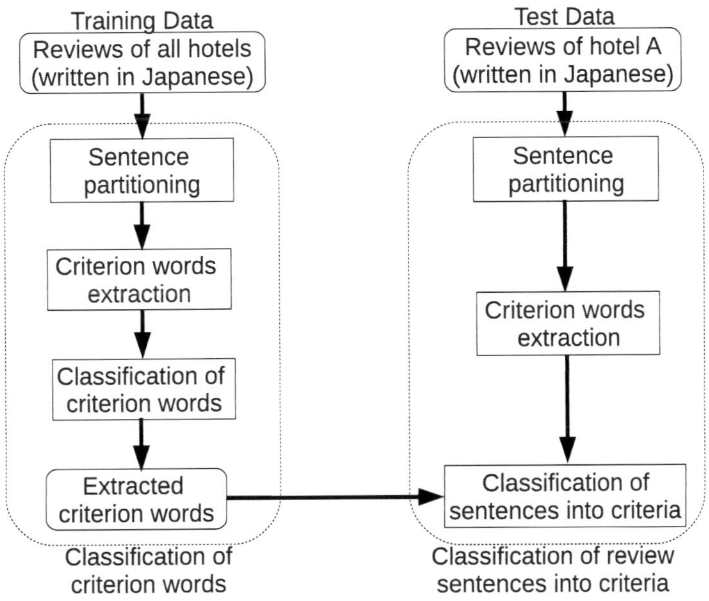

Figure 1: System overview.

4 Sentence partitioning

Compound sentences frequently appear in the reviews. Moreover, two or more criteria may be included within a compound sentence. For example, "The buffet-style breakfast is delicious, the room is also large and the scent of the shampoo and rinse in the bathroom are quite good": "(*chooshoku no baikingu mo oishiidesushi, heyamo hiroishi, ichiban kiniitteiruno ga heya ni oitearu shampuu to rinsu no kaori ga totemo iito omoimasu*)".

It is necessary to divide one sentence into some criteria. Fukushima proposed a method of sentence division for text summarization for TV news (Fukushima et al., 1999). They used rule based method for sentence partitioning. In this paper, each compound sentence was divided into some criteria by using compound sentence markers and "CaboCha" (Kudo and Matsumoto, 2002) which is a Japanese dependency structure Analyzer.

5 Criterion words extraction

Firstly, we defined criterion words as words that the reviewers notice in the reviews. Criterion words were frequently followed by postpositional particle: "*wa*" and adjective in the reviews written in Japanese. For extracting criterion words in reviews, we first extracted the pattern: "noun A + *wa* + adjective" from whole reviews. Next, we extracted "noun A", and finally, we collected words which are extracted as similar words of "noun A" by using the method mentioned in Section 6 and hypernym/hyponym of "noun A" in Japanese WordNet (Bond et al., 2009). Table 1 shows the adjectives which frequently appeared in the pattern: "noun A + *wa* + adjective".

Table 2 shows the extracted criterion words and their frequencies. These words in the table corresponds to criteria of the hotel.

Table 1: Adjectives which frequently appeared in "noun A + *wa* + adjective".

No	Adjective	Frequency	No	Adjective	Frequency
1	good (*yoi*)	142,719	6	delicious (*oishii*)	33,318
2	lack (*nai**)	73,186	7	inexpensive (*yasui*)	28,463
3	good (*yoi**)	67,643	8	delicious (*oishii**)	27,310
4	large(*hiroi*)	55,524	9	much (*ooi*)	23,122
5	near (*chikai*)	52,423	10	narrow (*semai*)	20,345

"*" indicates the word is written in hiragana.

Table 2: Candidate words of criteria (top 10).

No	Words	Frequency	No	Words	Frequency
1	room	56,888	6	service	11,270
2	breakfast	25,068	7	bath room	9,864
3	meal	17,107	8	noise	8,695
4	support	16,677	9	dish	8,252
5	location	14,866	10	hot spring	7,774

6 Similar word pair extraction

Reviews are written by many different people. People may express the same thing by using different expression. For example, "*heya*", "*oheya*" and "room" are the same sense, *i.e.*, room. Moreover, two words such as "*kyakushitsu*":(guest room) and "*heya*":(room) are often used in the same sense in the hotel review domain while those are different senses. Table 3 shows frequency of words which mean 'room' in a hotel review corpus.

Table 3: Extracted similar words of 'room'.

Words	Frequency
heya	171,796
oheya	38,547
room	17,203
kyakushitu	4,446

We thus collected similar words from hotel reviews by using Lin's method (Lin, 1998). Firstly, we extracted similar word pairs using dependency relationships. Dependency relationship between two words is used for extracting semantically similar word pairs. Lin proposed "dependency triple" (Lin, 1998). A dependency triple consists of two words: w, w' and the grammatical relationship between them: r in the input sentence. $||w, r, w'||$ denotes the frequency count of the dependency triple (w, r, w'). $||w, r, *||$ denotes the total occurrences of (w, r) relationships in the corpus, where "$*$" indicates a wild card.

We used three sets of Japanese case particles as r. Set A consists of two case particles: "*ga*" and "*wo*". They correspond to a subject and an object, respectively. Set B consists of six case particles. Set C consists of seventeen case particles. We selected word pairs which are extracted by using two or three sets.

For calculating similarity between w and w' with relation r, we used Formula (1).

$$I(w,r,w') = \log \frac{||w,r,w'|| \times ||*,r,*||}{||w,r,*|| \times ||*,r,w'||} \quad (1)$$

Let $T(w)$ be the set of pairs (r,w') such that $\log \frac{||w,r,w'|| \times ||*,r,*||}{||w,r,*|| \times ||*,r,w'||}$ is positive. The similarity $Sim(w_1,w_2)$ between two words: w_1 and w_2 are defined by Formula (2).

$$Sim(w_1,w_2) = \frac{\sum_{(r,w)\in T(w_1)\cap T(w_2)} (I(w_1,r,w) + I(w_2,r,w))}{\sum_{(r,w)\in T(w_1)} I(w_1,r,w) + \sum_{(r,w)\in T(w_2)} I(w_2,r,w)} \quad (2)$$

Table 4 shows the extracted similar word pairs.

Table 4: Results of extracting similar pairs using particle set A, B, C.

No.	Word1	Word2
1	favorable (*koukan*)	very favorable (*taihen koukan*)
2	route (*michizyun*)	route (*ikikata*)
3	stomach (*onaka*)	stomach (*onaka**)
4	dust (*hokori*)	dust (*hokori**)
5	net (net)	Internet (Internet)
6	renovation (*kaishu*)	renewal (renewal)
7	drain outlet (*haisuiguchi*)	drain (*haisuikou*)
8	word of mouth communication (*kuchikomi*)	word of mouth communication (*kuchikomi+*)
9	morning newspaper (*choukan*)	newspaper (*shinbun*)
10	a breakfast voucher (*choushokuken*)	ticket (ticket)

"*" indicates the word is written in hiragana.
"+" indicates the word is written in katakana.

In Table 4, there are some notational variants. In general, the pair of "morning newspaper" and "newspaper" and the pair of "breakfast voucher" and "ticket" are not the same meaning, while the two pairs are mostly the same sense in hotel reviews.

7 Classification of review sentences into criteria

We classified them into criteria by using lexical information of Japanese WordNet and similarity of words. We selected 12 criteria from the results shown in Table 2. Firstly, we classified each sentence into 12 criteria and miscellaneous as teaching data by hand. Next, we classified each sentence using two kind of Naive Bayes: multinomial Naive Bayes (MNB) and compliment Naive Bayes (CNB)(Rennie et al., 2003). Naive Bayes classifier is often used as a text classification because it is fast, easy to implement and relatively effective even if the training data is small. In the Naive Bayes classifier, we need a lot of training data per class. However, in this task, it is hard to collect many training data for some classes. We thus used CNB. CNB uses the compliment sets of each class for training, and it can be used more amount of data for each class. For expanding training data, we use sentences selected as same criterion by MNB and CNB. Table 5 shows classification results using MNB and CNB.

Table 5: Classification results using MNB and CNB.

Method	Precision	Recall	F-score
MNB	0.72	0.63	0.67
CNB	0.75	0.64	0.69
MNB&CNB	0.81	0.61	0.70

As we can see from Table 5 that when a sentence is classified into the same criterion by MNB and CNB, in most cases classified criterion is correct. Therefore, we used the sentences as additional training data.

Multinomial Naive Bayes classifier is obtained by using Formula (3).

$$MNB(d) = \arg\max_c \{\log \hat{p}(\theta_c) + \sum_i f_i \log \frac{N_{ci} + \alpha_i}{N_c + \alpha}\}, \quad (3)$$

where $\hat{}p(\theta_c)$ is the class prior estimate. j_i is the frequency count of word i in the reviews d. N_{ci} is number of times the word i appears in the training documents of class c. N_c is the number of words that appear in the training documents in class c. For α_i and α , we used 1 and the size of vocabulary, respectively. Similarly, CNB classifier is defined by Formula (4).

$$CNB(d) = \arg\max_c \{\log p(\vec{\theta}_c) - \sum_i f_i \log \frac{N_{\sim ci} + \alpha_i}{N_{\sim c} + \alpha}\}, \quad (4)$$

where $N_{\sim i}$ is the number of times word i occurred in documents in classes other than c and $N_{\sim c}$ is the total number of word occurrences in classes other than c, and α_i and α are smoothing parameters. $\vec{\theta}_c = \{\theta_{c1}, \theta_{c2}, ..., \theta_{cn}\}$.

8 Experiments and discussion

For the experiment, we used hotel review of Rakuten Travel [1]. Table 6 shows Review data of the Rakuten Travel.

Table 7 shows 12 criteria which we used in the experiments.

We classified each sentence into these 12 criteria and a miscellaneous cluster.

We used Japanese WordNet Version 1.1 (Bond et al., 2009) as Japanese Thesaurus dictionary. We employed Lin's method (Lin, 1998) for extracting similar word pairs in hotel reviews.

We conducted experiments for dividing reviews into every criterion. We used reviews of 5 budget hotels. The average number of review per hotel was 51.2. Table 8 shows the results of text segmentation.

[1] url= http://travel.rakuten.co.jp/ We used Rakuten travel review data provided by Rakuten Institute of Technology

Table 6: Reviews of Rakuten Travel.

amount of data	250MB
# of reviews	350,000
# of hotel	15437
# of words for each review	375
# of reviews for each hotel	23

Table 7: 12 Criteria and their criterion words.

No	Criteria	Criterion words	No	Criteria	Criterion words
1	location	location, access	7	bath	bath room, bathtub
2	facilities	swimming pool, massage chair	8	amenity	razor, toothbrush
3	service	support, service	9	network	Wi-Fi, broad band
4	meal	breakfast, meal	10	beverage	beer, coke
5	room	room, noise	11	bed	bed, pillow
6	lobby	lobby, lounge	12	parking lot	parking lot, car

As can be seen clearly from the Table 8, the results obtained by CNB are better than those obtained by MNB.

Table 8: Results of Clustering.

Method	Precision	Recall	F-score
MNB	0.74	0.65	0.69
CNB	0.76	0.67	0.71

We used two kinds of Naive Bayes classifiers: multinomial Naive Bayes (MNB) classifier and compliment Naive Bayes (CNB) classifier in the experiments. The results obtained by CNB were better than those obtained by MNB. One reason why the results obtained by the CNB method were better than those obtained by the MNB is that the difference number of words in the training data used in these methods, and the balance of the data within each class. The number of words in the training data used in the MNB was smaller than that of the CNB. Because we used the data which consists of the limited number of words corresponding to each criterion class. Therefore the number of the training data for each criterion class is different from each other. In contrast, the training data we used in the CNB consist of the complement words in each class. Thus, the number of words in the training data becomes larger than that of the MNB, and the training data itself becomes a well-balanced data with each class.

Conclusion

In this paper, we proposed a method for extracting criteria and their sentiment expression from hotel reviews. The results showed the effectiveness of our method. Future work will include: (i) extracting criterion words with high accuracy, (ii) applying the method to a large number of guests reviews for quantitative evaluation, (iii) applying the method to other data such as grocery stores: LeShop[2], TaFeng[3] and movie data: MovieLens[4] to evaluate the robustness of

[2]www.beshop.ch

[3]aiia.iis.sinica.edu.tw/index.php?option=com_docman&task=cat_view&gid=34&Itemid=41

[4]http://www.grouplens.org/node/73

the method.

Acknowledgements

The authors would like to thank the referees for their comments on the earlier version of this paper. This work was partially supported by The Telecommunications Advancement Foundation.

References

Beineke, P., Hastie, T., and Vaithyanathan, S. (2004). The sentimental factor : Improving review classification via human-provided information. In *the 42nd Annual Meeting of the Association for Computational Linguistics*.

Bond, F., Isahara, H., Uchimoto, K., Kuribayashi, T., and Kanzaki, K. (2009). Enhancing the japanese wordnet. In *The 7th Workshop on Asian Language Resources, in conjunction with ACL-IJCNLP*.

Fukushima, T., Ehara, T., and Shirai, K. (1999). Partitioning long sentences for text summarization. *Journal of Natural Language Processing (in Japanese)*, 6(6):131–147.

Hirao, T., Kitauchi, A., and Kitani, T. (2000). Text segmentation based on lexical cohesion and word importance. *Information Processing Society of Japan*, 41(SIG3(TOD6)):24–36.

Hu, M. and Liu, B. (2004). Mining opinion features in customer reviews. In *Proceedings of Nineteenth National Conference on Artifical Intelligence*.

Kudo, T. and Matsumoto, Y. (2002). Japanese dependency analysis using cascaded chunking. In *CoNLL 2002:Proceedings of the 6th Conference on Natural Language Learning 2002*, pages 63–69.

Lin, D. (1998). Automatic retrieval and clustering of similar words. In *Proceedings of 36th Annual Meeting of the Association for Computational Linguistics and 17th International Conference on Computational Linguistics Proceedings of the Conference*, pages 768–774.

Rennie, J. D. M., Shih, L., Teevan, J., and Karger, D. R. (2003). Tackling the poor assumptions of naive bayes text classifiers. In *Twentieth International Conference on Machine Learning*, pages 616–623.

Utiyama, M. and Isahara, H. (2001). A statistical model for domain-independent text segmentation. In *Proceedings of the 39th Annual Meeting on Association for Computational Linguistics*, pages 499–506.

Wei, W. and Gulla, J. A. (2010). Sentiment learning on product reviews via sentiment ontology tree. In *Annual Meeting of the Association for Computational Linguistics*, pages 404–413.

Yi, J. and Niblack, W. (2005). Sentiment mining in webfountain. In *Proceedings of the 21st International Conference on Data Engineering*.

Emotiphons: Emotion markers in Conversational Speech - Comparison across Indian Languages

Nandini Bondale[1] *Thippur Sreenivas*[2]
(1) School of Tech. and Comp. Sci., Tata Institute of Fundamental Research, Mumbai, 400005, India.
(2) Dept. of ECE, Indian Institute of Science, Bangalore, 560012, India.
drnandini.bondale@gmail.com, tvsree@ece.iisc.ernet.in

ABSTRACT

In spontaneous speech, emotion information is embedded at several levels: acoustic, linguistic, gestural (non-verbal), etc. For emotion recognition in speech, there is much attention to acoustic level and some attention at the linguistic level. In this study, we identify paralinguistic markers for emotion in the language. We study two Indian languages belonging to two distinct language families. We consider Marathi from Indo-Aryan and Kannada from Dravidian family. We show that there exist large numbers of specific paralinguistic emotion markers in these languages, referred to as *emotiphons*. They are inter-twined with prosody and semantics. Preprocessing of speech signal with respect to *emotiphons* would facilitate emotion recognition in speech for Indian languages. Some of them are common between the two languages, indicating cultural influence in language usage.

KEYWORDS : Emotion recognition, *emotiphons*, emotion markers, Indian languages

1 Introduction

One of the important reasons for communication is the desire on the part of the members to express their emotions (Millar 1951). Language is the effective tool to carry out this task and speech is the most efficient mode of language communication between humans. In the recent years, emotion recognition in human speech is more important because of human computer interaction as in automatic dialogue systems or robotic interactions (Cowie et al., 2001). In interactive applications, detection of emotions such as frustration, boredom or annoyance in the speaker's voice helps to adapt the system response, making the system more effective. Speech carries a lot of information over and above the text content in the language. Speaker's voice expresses the physical and emotional state, sex, age, intelligence and personality (Kramel, 1963). Emotion is intimately connected with cognition and many physiological indices change during emotion arousal (Lindsay and Norman, 1972). The task of speech emotion recognition is challenging as it is not clear which speech features are effective in distinguishing a large range and shades of emotions over a range of human voices and context. How a certain emotion is expressed generally depends on the speaker, his or her culture and environment (Ayadi et al., 2011). Therefore, integration of acoustic and linguistic information has been tried out. (Lee and Pieraccini, 2002, Schuller et al. 2004). Spoken dialogue and written language are very different due to many paralinguistic aspects such as the *emotiphons*, defined and discussed in this paper.

In this study, we examine specific lexical expressions in Indian languages conveying emotion, referred to as *emotiphons*. This is the first attempt of its kind to list and study these lexical expressions. We consider two Indian languages, namely Marathi from Indo-Aryan family and Kannada from Dravidian family, whose people are culturally very connected. This data across languages and their acoustic correlates would throw light on the flow of information from the prosodic level to the highest cognitive level of speech processing, in general, and emotional speech processing in particular.

The following section describes the role of *emotiphons* in emotion recognition. Section 3 lists *emotiphons* in Marathi and Kannada. Section 4 mentions the observations along with discussion. Section 5 states conclusions.

2 Speech and emotion

Cowie and Cornelius (2003) have described issues related to speech and emotion in great details, covering the basic concepts and relevant techniques to study conceptual approaches. It is well recognized that emotion analysis in human communication is multi-faceted and varied. It is also intertwined with the culture of the language users.

2.1 *Emotiphons*

In this study, we identify specific lexical expressions referred to as *Emotiphons*, used to communicate emotions, in Indian languages. *Emotiphons* are essentially short lexical expressions in conversational speech conveying emotions by modifying the prosody of the utterance. Use of *emotiphon* keeps the body of the lexical content unaltered in a sentence, but explicitly brings out the intended emotion. Yet they are not considered as part of lexicon always; hence can be referred to as paralinguistic markers. *Emotiphons* are analogous to emoticons of printed text that have become so essential in email communication. In contrast to affect-bursts which are non-speech in nature (Schroder 2003), *emotiphons* are phonetic in nature and blend well with the lexical phonetics and sentence structure of the language. Being short and specific, *emotiphons* disambiguate subtle emotions and help to convey emotions better and stronger.

2.2 Emotion recognition

In databases for emotion recognition, it is common to record the same sentence with different emotions, thus reducing the effect of lexical content on perceived emotions. This suggests that, a particular lexical content can be expressed in more than one type of emotion. In such cases, it can be seen from our data mentioned in section 3, that suitable *emotiphon* can be used by speakers, to effectively express the respective emotion.

Improvement in speech emotion recognition performance has been attempted by combining other information such as facial expressions or specific words along with acoustic correlates. It has been shown that searching for emotional keywords or phrases in the utterances and integrating linguistic classifier with acoustic classifier have improved emotion classification accuracy (Ayadi et al., 2011). Computational techniques used in these approaches could be varied depending on the sophistication of the system application. The *emotiphons* discussed in this paper would be an additional source for emotion recognition. The presence of *emotiphons* heavily affects the prosody and convey emotions effectively. Some of the *emotiphons* are stand-alone and hence may be identified through a pre-processing stage, such as keyword spotting, whereas other *emotiphons* would have to be viewed along with prosody. Stochastic model based recognition would be required in most cases, because of the subjective variability of pronunciation.

3 *Emotiphons* in two Indian Languages

The Indian subcontinent is a good example of a sprachbund (Emeneau, 1956), because there are two distinct language families, Indo-Aryan and Dravidian. However, there is a lot of interaction and similarity across the languages belonging to these two families due to centuries of language and culture contact. While grouping Indian languages using machine learning techniques, based on their text, it is observed that, Marathi is the closest language to the Southern zone consisting of the languages from Dravidian family and can be grouped with Hindi, Punjabi and Gujarati. The grouping corresponds well with the geographic proximity also (Ghosh et al., 2011).

In the following tables we give a sample list of *emotiphons* used in Marathi and Kannada, the languages of Maharashtra and Karnataka states respectively. We have categorized *emotiphons* in different groups. Phonetic representation of *emotiphons* is given using IPA symbols. Additional characteristics are mentioned wherever they are significant. (All the emotions mentioned in the following tables are indicative and may change from region to region where the language is spoken).

Table 1 lists the *emotiphons* that are smallest expressions consisting a single vowel or a diphthong. They are 'stand-alone' expressions, i.e., can be used in isolation to express the respective emotions and may not need conversation mode. In all the tables, 'K' stands for Kannada & 'M' and Marathi.

Phonetic representation	*Language*	*Pitch &/or loudness*	*Emotion description*
1. [ɑː] or [ɑ̃ː]	K& M	a) Falling b) Rising	a) Pain b) Request to repeat
2. [i]	K&M	Flat	Disgust, dislike
3. [ũː]	K&M	a) Falling b) Rising c) Low & louder	a) Exhausted b) Pain c) Disapproval
4. [e]	K&M	a) High b) Low	a) Rude alert b) Affectionate alert
5. [o]	K&M	a) Rising b) Flat	a) Exclamation b) Mild amazement
6. [ei]	K&M		Derogatory challenge

Table 1 - 'Stand-alone' *emotiphons*; (Vowels, diphthong)

Table 2 lists *emotiphons* which are fricative like and can be used as isolated expressions to express the respective emotion.

Phonetic representation	*Language*	*Additional characteristic*	*Emotion description*
1. [t͡ʃʰeː]	a) K b) M		a) Sadness b)Displeasure
2. [t͡ʃet͡ʃeː]	a) K b) M		a) Repenting b)Disapproval
3. a) [ʃiː] b) [cʰiː]	a) M b) K		Disgust
4. [ǀ] (dental click)	M	Single or multiple utterances with breaks	Frustration or repenting or disappointment or sadness

Table 2 - 'Stand-alone' *emotiphons;* (Fricatives, click)

Tables 3a and 3b list some of the *emotiphons* which involve multiple-phons.

Emotiphons in Table 3a can be used in isolation as in Table 1 and 2.

Phonetic representation	***Language***	***Additional characteristic***	***Emotion description***
1. [oho:]	K & M	a) No stress b) Stress 1st/last vowel	a) Surprise b)Surprise with sarcasm
2. [ohoho….]	K & M		Enjoying the surprise
3. [t̪ʰu]	K & M		Dirty, disgust
4. a) [əjjo:] b) [əjjəjjo:]	K		a) Pain b)Severe pain
5. [ɑigə:]	M		Pain
6. [ɑiggə:]	M		Boredom

Table 3a- 'Stand-alone' *emotiphons;* (Multi-phons)

Table 3b lists the multi-phon *emotiphons* that are used only in conversational mode in contrast to 'stand-alone' expressions.

Phonetic representation	***Language***	***Pitch or other characteristic***	***Emotion description***
1. [ə̃hə̃]	K&M		Emphatic disapproval, disagreement
2. a) [pɑpə] b) [ərere]	a) K b) M		Sympathy
3. a) [kəɳo] b) [re]	a) K b) M	Singular, masculine	Affectionate address
4. a) [kəɳe] b) [gə]	a) K b) M	Singular, feminine	Affectionate address

Table 3b – Conversation mode *emotiphons ;* (Multi-phons)

4 Observations and discussion

It can be seen from the tables above that the number of emotions covered by *emotiphons* are far more than those expressed in the databases mentioned in the literature for emotion recognition. Common emotions covered by the databases are anger, fear, joy, sadness, disgust, surprise and neutral, mainly in the prosody at the acoustic level. However, *emotiphons* express many more shades and nuances of emotions like affection, pain, disbelief, sympathy, boredom and so on, which are all important for the semantic context.

We have classified e*motiphons* grossly into three categories; Vowel like, Fricative like and Multi-phons as mentioned in Table 1, 2 and 3 respectively. *Emotiphons* in Table 1, 2 and 3a are 'Stand-alone', self-expressive, conveying a specific emotion. They are exclamatory in nature. 'Stand-alone' *emotiphons* are unaffected by the linguistic parameters such as gender and number. They cover large number of emotions. (All are not listed due to space limit). *Emotiphons* in Table 3b are used in conversation mode only.

Although we believe that many emotions would be common across all humans which is a Darvinian perspective (Hozjan and Kacic, 2003), we feel that expression of emotion is dependent on culture and society. As seen in Table 1 and 2, many *emotiphons* are common across Marathi and Kannada, suggesting that people using these languages share similar cultural values, although the languages belong to two different families. We feel that *emotiphons* would be common across other Indian languages too. (Study of *emotiphons* for other Indian languages is in progress). The common *emotiphons* across Marathi and Kannada are of 'stand-alone' type and are independent of linguistic parameters such as gender and number. *Emotiphons* which depend on linguistic parameters are expected to vary across the languages and is evident from Table 3b.

Conclusions

We identified that there exist many emotion markers, referred to as *emotiphons* in two Indian languages, Marathi and Kannada belonging to Indo-Aryan and Dravidian language family, respectively. We find that *emotiphons* are short lexical expression used in conversational speech to convey many different specific emotions explicitly and effectively. Although Marathi and Kannada are from two different language families, we notice that there are many common *emotiphons* across the two languages. Commonality of *emotiphons* across the languages would lead us to understand cognitive aspects of the emotion communication as well as the linguistic evolution. *Emotiphons* would play a major role in identification of emotion in speech processing, adding naturalness to synthesized speech, and in design of dialogue systems.

References

Ayadi, M. E., Kamel, M.S. and Karray, F. (2011). Survey on speech emotion recognition: features, classification schemes, and databases. *Pattern Recognition*, 44:572-587.

Cowie, R. and Cornelius, R. R. (2003). Describing the emotional states that are expressed in speech, *Speech Communication,* Vol. 40, pp 5-32.

Cowie, R., Douglas-Cowie, E., Tsapatsoulis, N., Kollias, S., Fellenz, W., and Taylor, J. (2001). Emotion recognition in human–computer interaction. *IEEE Signal Processing Magazine*, 18, 32–80.

Emeneau, M. B. (1956). India as a linguistic area. *Language*, Vol. 32, No. 1.

Ghosh, S. K. Girish, K. V. and Sreenivas, T. V. (2011). Relationship between Indian languages using long distance bigram language models, In *Proceedings of ICON-2011: 9th International Conference on Natural Language Processing,* pp 104-113, Macmillan Publishers, India.

Hozjan, V and Kacic, Z. (2003). Context-independent multi-lingual emotion recognition from speech signals. *Int. J. Speech Tech.,* 6:311-320.

Lee, C. and Pieraccini, R. Combining acoustic and language informationfor emotion recognition, In *Proceedings of the ICSLP 2002,* 873-876.

Kramel E. (1963). Judgment of personal characteristics and emotions from nonverbal properties of speech, *Psych. Bulletin,* 60:408-420.

Lindsay, P. H. and Norman, D. A. (1972). Human Information Processing, Academic Press, New York and London.

Millar, G. A. (1951). Language and Communication. McGraw-Hill Book Company, New York, U.S.

Schroder, M. (2003). Experimental study of affect bursts. *Speech Communication*, Vol. 40, pp 99-116.

Schuller, B., Rigoll G., Lang, M. (2004). Speech emotion recognition combining acoustic features and linguistic information in a hybrid support vector machine-belief network architecture, In *Proceedings of the ICASSP,* vol 1, pp.577-580.

How Humans Analyse Lexical Indicators of Sentiments- A Cognitive Analysis Using Reaction-Time

Marimuthu K and Sobha, Lalitha Devi

AU-KBC RESEARCH CENTRE, MIT Campus of Anna University, Chrompet, Chennai, India

marimuthuk@live.com, sobha@au-kbc.org

ABSTRACT

In this paper, we try to understand how the human cognition identifies various sentiments expressed by different lexical indicators of sentiments in opinion sentences. We use the psychological index, Reaction Time (RT) for the analysis of various lexical indicators required for understanding the sentiment polarity. The test bed was developed using linguistic categories of lexical indicators of sentiments and selected sentences which have various levels of sentiments. Experimental results indicate that variations in syntactic categories of the lexical indicators influence the thought in deciding sentiments at varied levels. The results from this work is to be used for fine tuning machine learning algorithms which are used for sentiment analysis and it can also be used in the development of real time applications such as educational tools to better educate students, particularly those with neurocognitive disorders.

KEYWORDS: Cognition, Syntactic Categories, Reaction-Time, Lexical Indicators, Sentiment Analysis

1 Introduction

Sentiment analysis and opinion mining have gained importance in research for the last several years, giving emphasis on classification of opinions in movie and product reviews. Sentiments are expressed in a text through two ways, 1) explicitly marked lexical indicators and 2) implicitly carried out through non-evaluative and non-visibly subjective statements such as sarcasm. Sentiment analysis is a process to identify the opinion of a statement. The analysis is done by various disciplines such as linguistics, cognitive science, computational linguistics etc.

Our goal is to find the level of cognition associated with various syntactic categories of lexical indicators of sentiments in opinion sentences. Generally, the syntactic categories of words vary depending on the context in which they appear in a sentence. And specifically, in sentiments, the lexical indicators can have different Part-Of-Speeches (POS) as the sentence construction may vary depending on the reviewers' writing style. On analysing various sentiments, we found that lexical indicators commonly associate themselves with four syntactic categories i.e. adjective(ADJ), adverb(ADV), noun(N), and verb(V). In our study, we consider only these lexical indicators which bring out sentiments of statements. Analysis further brought in that is lexical indicators inherently intensifies the sentiments at varied levels. Consider the following examples.

1. *one of the greatest family-oriented fantasy-adventure movies.*

Here, "*greatest*" which is an adjective acts as a positive sentiment-indicating word.

2. *unfortunately, the story and the actors are served with a hack script.*

Here, "*hack script*" which is a noun acts as negative sentiment-indicating words.

Each of the above statements has a lexical indicator which acts as a stimulus for deciding the polarity of the snippet. But, the level of cognition required to identify and comprehend the stimulus varies with various syntactic categories among various participants. So, we concentrate to find this varied level of cognition using our psychological experimentation.

2 Literature Survey

Sentiment analysis is a thrust area in computational linguistics and different approaches such as heuristics based, linguistic rules based, statistical based, machine learning based, and cognitive methods, are used to classify sentiments.

At linguistics level, sentiments can be extracted from a sentence using various approaches like lexicon based approach, exploiting morphological features, semantic orientation of individual words etc. One typical example is a contextual intensifier. (Polanyi and Zaenen, 2004) defined contextual intensifiers as lexical items that weaken or strengthen the base valence of the term modified. The work by (Benamara et al., 2006) determine the importance of syntactic category combinations in opinions. They suggest that adjective and adverb combinations are better than adjectives alone in determining the strength of subjective expressions within a sentiment sentence.

At Rule-based level, polarity prediction depends mainly on hand-coded rules. Class Sequential Rules (CSR) had been studied in the work of (Luke K.W. Tan, 2011) and generalized polarity prediction rules were introduced that allows polarity rules to be applied across different domains.

Statistical approaches involve implementation of machine learning algorithms for sentiment classification. Performance of three machine learning methods (Naïve Bayes, Maximum Entropy classification, and Support Vector Machines) for sentiment classification of movie reviews had been analysed by (Pang et al., 2002). They concluded that these methods do not perform as well on sentiment classification as on traditional topic based categorization. Most prior work on the specific problem of categorizing expressed opinionated text had focussed on binary classification i.e. positive vs. negative(Turney, 2002; Pang et al., 2002; Dave et al., 2003; Yu et al., 2003).

At the cognitive level, (Ignacio Serrano et al., 2009) had tried to simulate high level cognitive processes in human mind. Their model relied on semantic neural network to build a cognitive model for human reading. Further, it is well known from (Saul Sternberg, 2004) that human reading is a process of sequential perception over time during which the brain builds mental images and inferences which are reorganized and updated until the end of the text. While reading a text, these mental images will help people to relate similar texts, extract, and classify them. The dependence between cognitive linguistics and sentiments, its metaphor and prototypical scenario, and various sentiments or emotions briefed in (Ignacio Serrano et al., 2009).

In this work, our main aim is to understand how various syntactic categories influence sentiment prediction and we find this using RT index. The rest of the paper is organized as follows. Section 3 discusses reaction time opinion mining experiment. Section 4 explains results, graphical representation, and comparison of various syntactic categories. Section 5 focuses on the inferences drawn from results. Section 6 explains major problems encountered in our experiment. In section 7 we give a detailed discussion on results and in final section we conclude by giving future work directions.

3 Reaction Time Opinion Mining Experiment

3.1 Definition

Reaction Time (RT; also called response time or latency) is the time taken to complete a task by a human. Specific to our goal, RT is the total time taken by a participant to read an opinion sentence, interpret the sentiment polarity and record the choice. In general, there are two parameters in this experiment, Recognition RT and Choice RT. Recognition RT is the time in which the subjects should respond and Choice RT is the time in which the subjects have to select a response from a set of possible responses. In our experiment, each obtained RT represents a combination of Recognition and Choice RT.

3.2 Input Data Description

For our experiment, we had used the publicly available Pang et al. movie review corpus. The data set had 5331 positive-polarity snippets and 5331 negative-polarity snippets. The data is clean i.e. contained only English language text. From this dataset, we took 1000 unique snippets i.e. 500 from positive-polarity and 500 from negative-polarity category. Since we consider only four syntactic categories (ADJ, ADV, N, and V), each syntactic category will have 125 unique positive and negative snippets. Based on the POS of lexical indicator of snippets, each snippet (positive or negative) in input dataset is manually classified into one of the four categories until we reach a total count of 250 snippets (125 positive and 125 negative) for each category.

3.3 Set data Preparation and Representation

In each category, snippets are manually marked either as simple or complex opinion based on the number of words. A set of 20 opinions is prepared for every participant. In order to maintain a constant measuring factor among various participants' RT values, and to provide a blend of varying difficulty level opinions and also to avoid mere guessing of sentiment polarity, six different techniques are followed while forming an opinion set. 1) First, each set has equal number of simple and complex opinions from positive and negative category and none of the same category opinions are displayed to participants in a follow-up fashion. 2) Second, the count of all syntactic categories is maintained at a fixed ratio so that Mean and SD measurements are not biased. Hence, for a set with 20 snippets, each category's snippet count will be 5 i.e. 5ADJs, 5ADVs, 5Ns, 5Vs. 3) Third, the sentiment polarity count is also maintained at a fixed ratio to maintain a balance between both polarity categories. So, in a set with 20 snippets, each polarity's count will be 10. 4) Fourth, none of the same polarity snippets are displayed in a consecutive manner throughout the test. This is to avoid mere guessing of sentiment polarities. 5) Fifth, snippets are jumbled in a random fashion so that no two snippets of same syntactic category follow one another. 6) Sixth, snippets in a particular set will not be repeated in any other set.

3.4 Experimental Setup and RT Measurement

The system design is an important factor in RT measurement and its importance is emphasized in (Saul Stemberg, 2004). While designing the user interfaces of RT system, stimulus design considerations specified in (Saul Stemberg, 2004) such as large displays, minimized noise etc., had been strictly followed. This is to confirm that these factors should not make the user uncomfortable during the test thereby affecting RTs in an adverse manner which is not desirable. To accurately measure RT, we also strictly adhered to the following design considerations. At any given moment during the testing time, only one sentiment snippet is shown at the top of the webpage along with a running timer at top right corner of the page. The polarity choice buttons are always placed nearer to the end of snippets to attenuate any millisecond delay that will be caused when moving the cursor away from snippets towards the buttons. The cut-off time for answering each snippet in question is *15s* after which the timer will expire. Providing cut-off time is to measure the precise RT which can be set depending upon the task. It is also to attenuate the effect of overtime which otherwise would make the final graph skewed. The timer runs separately for each snippet. So, the participants can take as much time as needed before navigating to next snippet but they are not advised to do so. The number of snippets per participant is limited to 20 so that they will not get bored which otherwise will affect the RT adversely (Saul Sternberg, 2004). We developed a web-based system to collect and record response time.

A participant begins the test by reading the rules. Then s/he enters the testing session and starts answering the choices for all 20 snippets in the given set. The RT values of each snippet will be automatically recorded in a database which will be retrieved later for further analysis. This procedure is repeated for all 50 participants and the corresponding RT values are recorded. Ideal state of a participant is a condition in which s/he mentally reacts normally under normal circumstances and is also devoid of any serious physical or mental disorder that degrades Intelligent Quotient (IQ) level.

3.5 Evaluation

We calculated mean and SD values for our statistical RT analysis. Prior to calculation of these values, we have considered three cases of RT values i.e. *Raw case, Correct case,* and *Wrong case*. *Raw case* contains RTs of both correctly predicted and wrongly predicted opinions i.e. true positive, false positive, true negative, and false negative. *Correct case* contains only the RTs of correctly predicted opinions out of the given set i.e. true positive and true negative. *Wrong case* contains only the RTs of wrongly predicted opinions out of the given set i.e. false positive and false negative.

4 Experimental Results

The calculated Mean and SD of various RT values are tabulated here. The measured RT values are in centiseconds (cs). 10millisecond=1cs

Syntactic Category	Positive Opinion		Negative Opinion	
	SD	**Mean**	**SD**	**Mean**
Adjective	128.796	350.89	204.619	415.10
Adverb	181.545	383.50	211.351	432.58
Noun	190.602	454.84	238.067	506.73
Verb	180.740	450.97	219.593	455.77

TABLE 1 – Mean & SD values for Correct Case.

4.1 Graphical Representation of RT for various Syntactic Categories

In all the graphs depicted here, only some sample snippets in each case are plotted in x-axis and the corresponding atomic RT values are plotted in y-axis. For a given syntactic category, the atomic RT comparison is done only with snippets of similar difficulty category i.e. simple positive vs. simple negative and complex positive vs. complex negative.

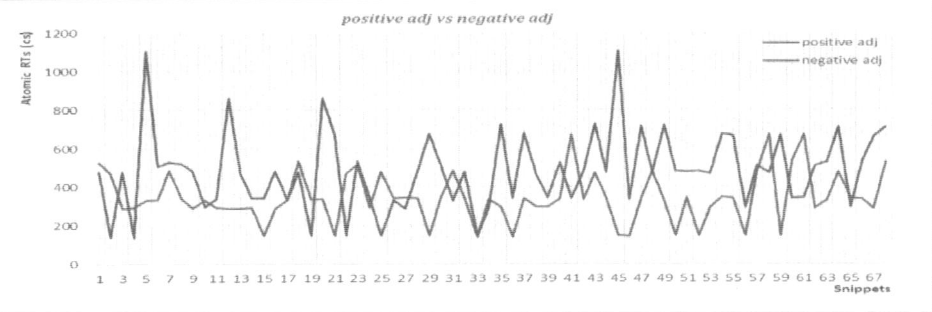

FIGURE 1 *Snippets vs. RTs* for Correct Case (pos-adj & neg-adj comparison)

From Fig.1, we can infer that there is an appreciable variation in RT for each positive and negative adjective snippet.

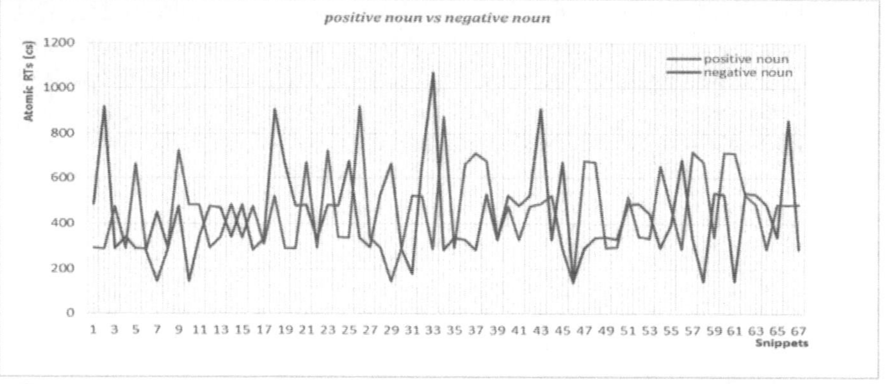

FIGURE 2 *Snippets vs. RTs* for Correct Case (pos-noun & neg-noun comparison)

The Correct Case Noun chart (Fig.2) indicates not many differences in RT values of positive and negative noun snippets. But slight variation exists which further suggests some participants struggled with positive opinions while most others struggled with negative opinions for this category.

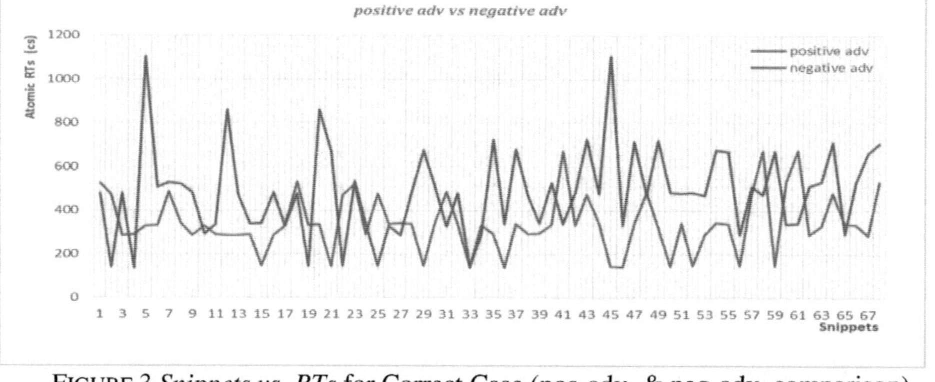

FIGURE 3 *Snippets vs. RTs* for Correct Case (pos-adv. & neg-adv. comparison)

Fig.3 graph clearly shows the observable differences in the RT values. On comparing this with Noun chart (Fig.2), the curve in this graph shows a clear difference in atomic RT values which also suggests its difficulty level. Analysing Fig.4 yields the inference that there is not much variation in RT with some snippets but considerable difference still with other snippets.

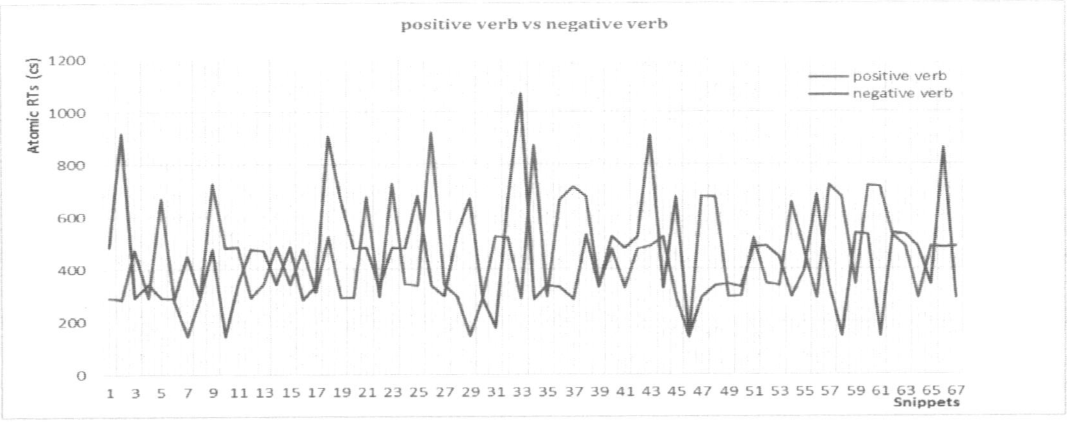

FIGURE 4 *Snippets vs. RTs* for Correct Case (pos-verb & neg-verb comparison)

5 Inferences

Interesting inferences and conclusions are derived from the analysis of above graphs and the Mean RT values. Irrespective of syntactic category, negative polarities are more difficult to predict than positive polarities i.e. participants take more time (slow RT) to recognize negative polarity than positive polarity. This is concluded by comparing Mean, and atomic RT values of positive and negative snippets of equal difficulty level (simple-simple or complex-complex opinion). In both positive and negative category opinions, polarity prediction is relatively easy when lexical indicators in a snippet has an *ADJ* syntactic category than the one with an adverbial or other category.The above inference implies that brain's perception is quick in polarity identification when sentiments contain the syntactic category *ADJs*. But, it is relatively slow for other syntactic categories with the highest level of difficulty (slower RT) corresponding to *NOUN* category. It is also evident from Wrong Case RT measure that people commit mistakes relatively often in the case where *ADVs* and *NOUNs* serves as lexical indicators (sentiment-indicating words) in positive opinions and *ADVs and VERBs* in negative opinions. This implies that people are easily deceived by the usage of *negated adverbial and verb* category than other negated syntactic categories.

6 Participants and Problems faced

The present study had been experimented among Indian students who learned English as a second language and were almost at graduation level (age group range 20-23). They faced difficulties mainly because of second language phenomenon. Particularly, they had struggled due to the usage of hard vocabulary and movie jargon words in sentiments. To get an insight of the difficulty level, consider the following opinion snippets,

3. *"a screenplay more ingeniously constructed than " memento " " (ingeniously-deceiving and hard vocabulary)*

7 Discussion

In rare cases, participants missed polarity detection within allotted time. The actual reason is not clear and to detect that further investigations are essential. We tried to find the reason by seeking feedback from test taking population. In that, they had expressed their difficulty in understanding the semantics of highly complex and jargoned nature of the movie reviews within 15s. In an effort to study and mitigate this problem, trained RT test is conducted. Initially, some participants are trained with some sample set of snippets for polarity identification. Then, the RT values of these participants are measured for a variety of different set of snippets. On comparing the trained test RT values with previously obtained RT values, we found that time taken for every snippet had been slightly reduced (quick RT). This reduction in RT is due to the training tests taken. One of the four truths mentioned in (Saul Sternberg, 2004) states that RT diminishes with practice. So, for the precise measurement of RT values, factors such as mock tests, training, giving hints etc. should be carefully considered when designing an RT system.

Conclusion & Future Work

The level of cognition associated with various syntactic categories is found. The comparative analysis of various syntactic categories had been done and valuable inferences were drawn. We also arrived at a representation of difficulty level for the considered syntactic categories. It is evident from the results that *adjective* category requires very less RT than other considered syntactic categories. So, *adjective* category will serve as a better stimulus (quick RT) than *adverb or noun or verb*. This finding can be incorporated in the development of better educational tools to better educate students particularly those with neurocognitive disorders. Future work will focus on incorporating the findings of this work into machine learning algorithms which can then be used for automated sentiment classification task. This may help to improve the accuracy of sentiment prediction which will make these algorithms intelligent and also fast in sentiment classification.

Acknowledgments

We thank Department of Computer Science, Cornell University for providing the movie review dataset and the student participants who had helped us with RT test. We also thank the reviewers for their insightful comments.

References

Bo Pang and Lillian Lee. (2008). *Opinion Mining and Sentiment Analysis*, Foundations and Trends in Information Retrieval Vol. 2, Nos. 12, 1135

Bo Pang and Lillian Lee, Shivakumar Vaithyanathan. (2002). *Thumbs up? Sentiment Classification using Machine Learning Techniques*, Proceedings of EMNLP 2002, pp. 79-86

Farah Benamara, Carmine Cesarano, Antonio Picariello, Diego Reforgioto, VS Subrahmanian. (2006). *Sentiment Analysis: Adjectives and Adverbs are better than Adjectives Alone*, International Conference on Weblogs and Social Media, Boulder, Colorado, U.S.A

http://www.sbl-site.org/publications/article.aspx?articleId=660

Ignacio Serrano, J., Dolores del Castillo, M., and Iglesias, A. (2009). *Dealing with written language semantics by a connectionist model of cognitive reading,* Neurocomputing 72, 713725.

Judith Tonhauser. (2000). *An Approach to Polarity Sensitivity and Negative Concord by Lexical Underspecification,* Proceedings of the 7th International HPSG Conference, UC Berkeley.

Luke K.W. Tan, Jin-Cheon Na and Yin-Leng Theng, Kuiyu Chang. (2011). *Phrase-level sentiment polarity classification using rule-based typed dependencies*, In proceedings of SWSM'11, China.

Michael Israel. (1996). *Polarity Sensitivity as Lexical Semantics,* In Linguistics and Philosophy, pp. 619-666.

Miller, C. A. and G. H. Poll. (2009). *Response time in adults with a history of language difficulties.* Journal of Communication Disorders 42(5): 365-379

Paula Chesley, Bruce Vincent, Li Xu, and Rohini K. Srihari. (2006). *Using Verbs and Adjectives to Automatically Classify Blog Sentiment.* National Conference on Artificial Intelligence-Spring Symposium, AAAI Press, pp. 27-29.

Perfetti, C.A. (1999). *Comprehending written language: a blue print of the reader*, in: Brown, C., Hagoort, P. (Eds.), The Neurocognition of Language, Oxford University Press, Oxford, pp. 167208.

Pyhala R, Lahti J, Heinonen K, Pesonen A.K., Strang-Karlsson S, Hovi P, Jarvenpaa A.L., Eriksson J.G., Andersson S, Kajantie E,Raikkonen K. (2011). *Neurocognitive abilities in young adults with very low birth weight*, Neurology, December 6, 201177:2052-2060

Robert Whelan. (2008). *Effective analysis of reaction time data*, The Psychological Record, 58, 475-482.

Sternberg, S. (1969). *The discovery of processing stages: Extensions of Donders' method. In W.G. Koster (Ed.), Attention and performance II. Acta Psychologica, 30, 276-315*

Saul Sternberg. (2004). *Reaction-Time Experimentation, Proseminar in Psychological Methods*, Psychology 600-301, spring semester.

Yang Mu, Dacheng Tao. (2010). *Biologically inspired feature manifold for gait recognition,* Neurocomputing 73, 895902.

A PILOT STUDY OF HINDUSTANI MUSIC SENTIMENTS

VELANKAR M.R.[1], *SAHASRABUDDHE H.V.*[2]

1. Cummins College Of Engineering, Karvenagar, Pune
2. Retired from IIT, MUMBAI

makarand.velankar@cumminscollege.in, hvs_buddhe@hotmail.com

ABSTRACT

Music is a universal language to convey sentiments. Hindustani classical music (HCM) has a long tradition and people from various cultural backgrounds are fascinated by it. Each performance of a given raga in HCM is supposed to create a common mood among most listeners. We have selected solo instrumental clips of bamboo flute for pilot study. We have chosen one instrument in order to eliminate the effect of words in vocal and effect of different timbres. We selected 2 ragas and 3 clips of each raga to understand possible sentiments created. We had total 4 sessions with 20 novice listeners and played 2 clips per session. Listeners have given rating for 13 sentiments on a numeric scale. From the Listener's feedback, we have stated our own observations about the sentiment creation. General sentiments felt by novice Indian listeners were found similar to the expected mood of specific raga.

1 Introduction

Communication is done via two modes such as verbal and non verbal communication. Verbal forms such as speech, talk or non verbal form such as letter, email, SMS are means of communication used with specific purpose. The purpose of such communication may be just to inform someone, without any specific sentiments involved in it. Verbal communication like a technical session by the instructor to students does fall under same category. In such communications, sentiments may or may not get conveyed along with matter to the listeners or target audience.

People do use different means such as body language during talk or impact on specific words during speech to convey specific sentiments. In written communication, use of specific words, exclamation marks etc. can be used to express the sentiments. Since many years, the sentiments are also conveyed in abstract way using different art forms such as music, dance, drawings etc.

In Music, a performer or composer conveys certain feelings or sentiments to the listener through musical language. Music is considered as universal language to express sentiments as it does not require understanding of any specific spoken or written language. Each musical form has its own ways of expressing sentiments. A performer or composers convey the sentiments according to their own perceptions considering target audience. They use different means such as tunes, instruments, voice, rhythms and their combination to convey sentiments. They can have different styles or different school of thoughts to express music.

If we compare music with natural language, we find similarities of structure. However, semantics of our language is designed to communicate information, thoughts, ideas, whereas semantics of music are aesthetic. The following mapping constitutes our hypothesis (Table 1).

Ingredient	**Natural**	**(Raga) Music**
Fundamental unit	Alphabets	Swars/notes
Smallest unit with	Words	Phrases of 2 or more melodic notes
Smallest complete unit	Sentence	Avartan or multiple phrases together with indication of conclusion / start.

Table 1 -Mapping Hypothesis

In the Indian performing arts, a rasa is an emotion inspired in an audience by a performer. They are described by Bharata Muni in the Natyasastra, an ancient work of dramatic theory. We generally observe Sringaram or love, Karunyam or tragedy, Shantam or peaceful, bhakti or spiritual devotion are prominently observed sentiments in Indian Music. It is generally very difficult to represent all feelings or sentiments in exact words. User created tags with exhaustive vocabulary can be possible solution for individual expression of sentiments.

In case of music, there are many factors responsible for sentiments creation. We can classify them in two broad categories as listener's perspective or felt sentiments and performer or composer's perspective or expected sentiments. Listener's background about specific music form, attention towards different musical features, specific mind set etc. are important factors in listener's perspective. Musical contents such as the notations played in specific musical clip, specific musical phrases, tempo, timbre, instrumentation, ornamentation etc. are factors from performer or composer's perspective. Sentiments can be conveyed in actual performance using different techniques such as emphasis on specific musical phrases, proper use of pauses, voice modulations etc.

2 Related work

Martin Clayton makes the following points in his article "Towards a theory of musical meaning" (Clayton 2001):

- Musical experience depends on our attention primarily on auditory information and perhaps in the extent to which sound information is understood in a non-linguistic mode.
- Each individual perceives and decodes the information differently. Thus the meaning or experience is always experience to someone.
- There are many more ways in which musical experiences are meaningful. Auditory information can be understood metaphorically as patterned movement independently of its parsing into elemental notes.

We need to recognize that musical experience is meaningful in a variety of ways, that these ways are interconnected, and that the relationships between different dimensions of meaning are important.

Achyut Godbole (Godbole 2004) has discussed expressions created from different ragas in Hindustani music. Raga is a framework of rules for building melody, which has the power to produce many similar-sounding melodies. The art music of Northern India, known as Hindustani classical music (HCM) has evolved to its present form over at least the last 600 years. Bhatkhande (1957) mentioned about the conventions for raga and documented different compositions in ragas. HCM Raag-mala (2004) has thrown more light on current practice of raga performance. A "raga" in HCM (roughly a mode) is supposed to create a common expression among listeners.

Kai Tuuri (2007) defined different modes of listening. Active listening involves scenarios such as concerts. In case of passive listening, listener is generally involved in doing some other primary activity along with listening music in the background. Different emotional models such as 7 keyword mood model used by Yi Liu (2009) for Chinese classical music or Thayer's 2-D emotional model widely used by music researchers have attempted to model listener's emotions in different ways.

3 Preliminary work

The sentiments created by music in different listeners, or even the same listener at different times, may vary. The response of a listener depends on many factors such as cultural background, upbringing, mood of the listener and individual likes and dislikes as factors related to individuals. The response is also dependent on the attention of the listener towards timbre of voice or instrument, notes played, tempo and rhythm in the clip. Although it is difficult to catch the common expressions from any music form, we have attempted to find, as far as it is possible, the common sentiments created by HCM on Indian listeners with similar cultural background. Meaning or expression from music can be entirely different depending on the focus of the listener. Sentiments perception is subjective to every individual in any music form.

HCM has a long tradition and people from various cultural backgrounds are fascinated by it. Each performance of a given raga in HCM is supposed to create a common sentimental mood among most listeners. HCM has evolved to its present form over at least 600 years. The khyal form of vocal music and instrumental presentation mimicking vocal styles are relatively recent developments in HCM. We have chosen instrumental music as we intend to associate sentiments perceived to listeners with composition of raga.

We have selected one wind instrument Bansuri or Bamboo Flute for our study of sentiments. Bansuri has also long history and is also associated with lord Krishna in Hindu religion. In recent years, artist like Pandit Pannalal Ghosh, Pandit Hariprasad Chaurasiya etc. are the main contributors for popularizing Basuri among HCM listeners. We have chosen 2 ragas - Marubihag and Marwa - for our initial sessions as the two are perceived to create different sentimental moods. Marubihag is supposed to create happy and excited mood whereas Marwa is supposed to create sad and depressed mood. It is very difficult to extract the sentiments in exact words. We attempted to find the possible sentiments for the musical clips selected from the seasoned listeners. This exercise provided us many possible keywords or tags with synonyms to represent sentiments. Figure 2 shows the distinct sentiments referred by seasoned listeners, which we used for the experiments.

A	Happy	H	Surrender
B	Exciting	I	Love
C	Satisfaction	J	Request
D	Peaceful	K	Emotional
E	Graceful	L	Pure
F	Gentle	M	Meditative
G	Huge		

Figure 2– Sentiments list

4 Experiments for sentiments extraction

We decided to use novice Indian listeners as subjects in our sessions to understand the sentiments created from the raga music, since seasoned listeners have their predefined mindsets built through listening to raga music for years and knowledge of convention. We have discussed with Pandit Keshav Ginde (Ginde 2011), renowned bansuri player, about the sentiments associated with ragas, use of gamakas (inflexions in notes) and his own experience while presenting specific ragas. We discussed about features of bansuri performances and perceived feedback from the listeners. He advised us about suitable duration and presentation of performance considering the listener's level and background.

The HCM performance usually has 3 parts: first alap, followed by vilambit (slow tempo) or Madhya laya (medium tempo) and finally drut laya (fast tempo) presentation. In alap, raga notes are played or sung with slow tempo to build the atmosphere at the beginning. During alap, there is no rhythm accompaniment.

We selected 3 clips of each raga. Out of these 3 clips, we had one clip each of alap, Madhya laya and drut laya. Generally duration of alap and drut laya is small as compared to Madhya or Vilambit laya during the performance. We selected all clips of duration of about 2 to 3 minutes regardless of the duration of the corresponding section in the performance. We selected the duration of 2 to 3 minutes considering the attention span of novice listeners and an assumption of the minimum time required to generate the sentiments.

After getting feedback about possible patience of novice listeners to listen classical music, we decided to play 2 melodies per session with a gap of about 5 minutes between two melodies. We decided to play clips with similar tempo in each session to eliminate the effect of comparative tempo difference during session. We had total 4 sessions with about 20 listeners in each session. Out of 4 sessions, two sessions were for Madhya laya (medium tempo) considering the total duration of Madhya laya during performance.

5 Observations from the experiments

Since most of the listeners were in the age group of 18-20 with almost no exposure to HCM, we kept an open mind about the outcome of the sessions. We gave them a brief introduction before the session, explaining the objective of session and how to fill the feedback forms. This exercise helped us to bring the mind sets of all listeners into a common mode of listening and to experience the mood created from the clip.

Listeners gave rating to different sentiments on the scale of 0 to 100. For example most happy can be 100 and most sad can be 0 for the sentiment "happy". Listeners expressed their experience in their own words in addition to rating the given list of sentiments. We also held personal discussions with some of the listeners to understand the effectiveness of the session and understand their view points about listening music. The exercise of discussion after session has given us insight into thought processes of youth representatives.

We have presented comparative data for 2 ragas Marwa and Marubihag (MB) in 4 different charts as Madhya laya, Alap, Drut and overall data (Appendix). Chart values represent average response of all listeners for respective sentiments on the numeric scale 0-100. We can analyze various sentimental parameters at different tempos for 2 ragas in 3 charts and overall data represents averages of all responses to our selected ragas.

We have observed the pattern for each sentiment for all charts. Marubihag is perceived as happier in all compare to Marwa except in the case of drut responses where both are perceived as equally happy. Marubihag is perceived as more exciting and graceful than Marwa in all tempos. Marwa is appeared as huge and creating stronger feeling about surrender, love, satisfaction, purity and peace compare to Marubihag except during fast tempo clips. Marwa is considered to convey request and emotions more than Marubihag except in Madhya laya. Marwa was considered to be more meditative than Marubihag except during alap. Marwa is perceived as sadder and more pleading as compared to Marubihag. This is most prominent in the response to alap and Madhya laya clips.

Listener's attention towards rhythm in drut laya can be major factor for change in pattern in many sentiments for drut laya. During drut session, Order of clips can have some impact on sentiments in drut and alap sessions. Fast tempo seems to be the most important factor in creating "excitement". Overall sentiments perceived by novice listeners were analogous to the raga sentiments expected as per seasoned listeners.

Conclusions

Shudhdha note prominence in raga maru bihag reflects happy mood and komal note prominence in marwa reflects sad sentiments. This is similar to major and minor chords in the western music and their possible association with emotions. Tempo of the music along with notations do play major role in sentiments creation. Faster tempo will reflect in more excitement. Expected sentiments in the domain of composers or performer perspective can be common whereas felt emotions is individual or subjective domain of listener may be different. For similar musical background listeners, the sentiments felt for familiar musical form will be generally similar for specific musical clip.

Future work

We have plans to conduct similar sessions with clips of different ragas, and other sessions with clips in the same raga with wider range of instruments to verify our observations about raga and observe inter-instrumental differences. We are of the view to conduct sessions with clips of different duration to verify our assumption about the minimum time span required to affect the mood of the listener. We plan to conduct more experiments with smaller duration clip with specific musical phrases to associate possible sentiments with musical phrases.

References

Pandit Vishnunarayan Bhatkhande (1957). Kramik pustak malika-part 1 to 6 *Hathras: Sangeet Karyalaya 1st edition.*

Dr. Martin Clayton (2001). Towards a theory of musical meaning *British Journal of ethnomusicology vol-10/I.*

Achyut Godbole, Sulbha Pishvikar (2004). Nadvedh *Rajhauns prakashan*, 2004.

Keshav Ginde, (2011). Private discussion, August 2011.

Kai Tuuri, Manne-Sakari Mustonen, Antti Pirhonen (2007). Same sound – Different meanings: A Novel Scheme for Modes of Listening *Audio Mostly September 27-28 Germany.*

The Raag-mala music society of Toronto (2004). *The Language of Indian Art Music Toronto.*

Yi Liu, Yue Gao (2009). Acquiring mood information from songs in large music databases.

Appendix

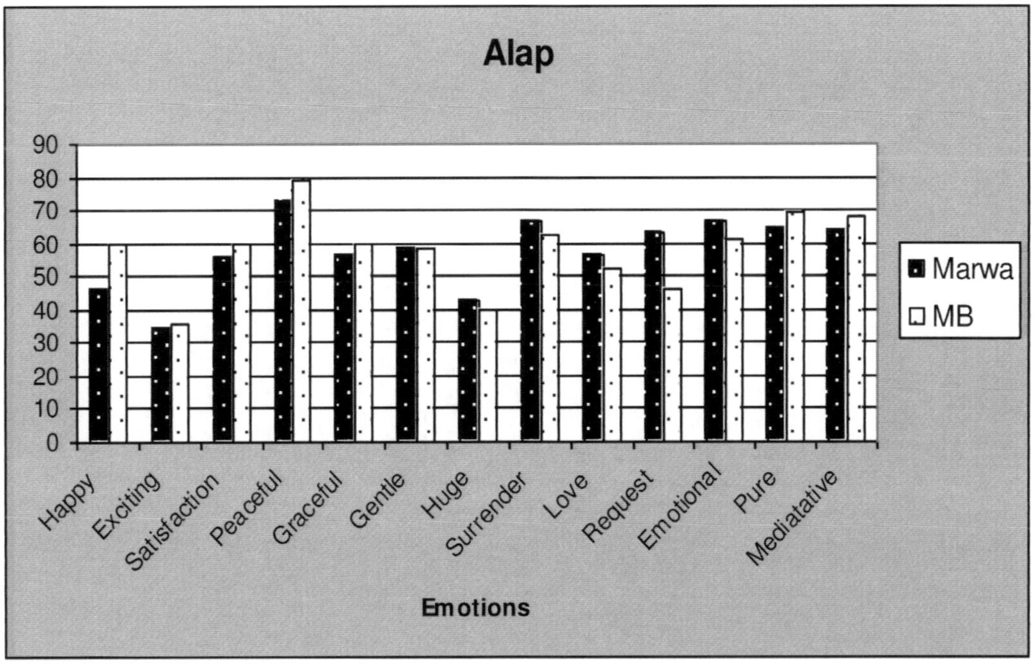

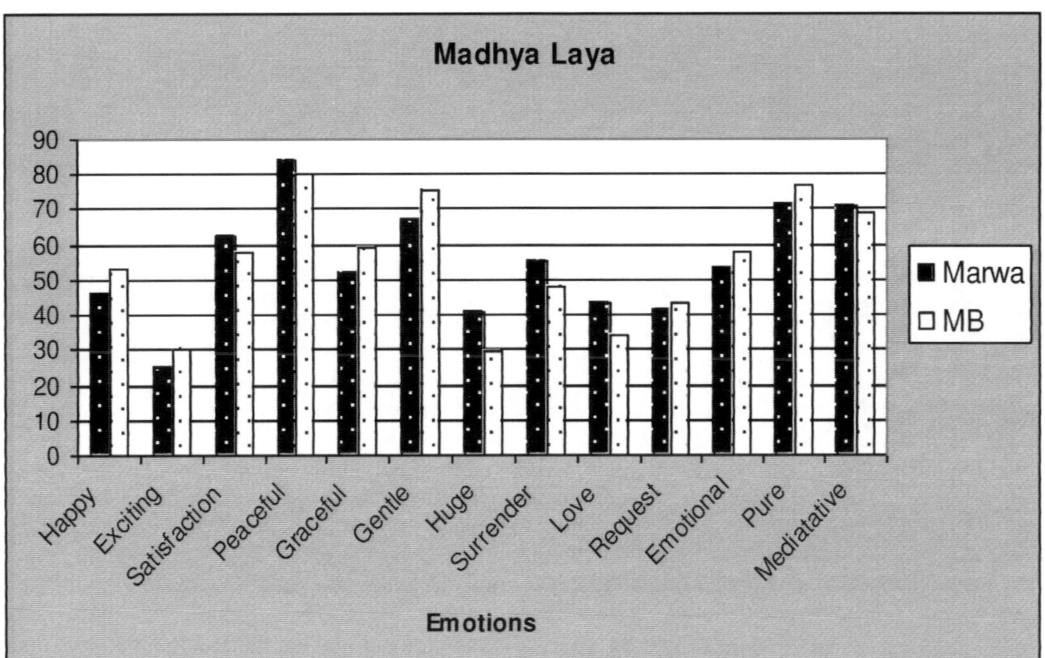

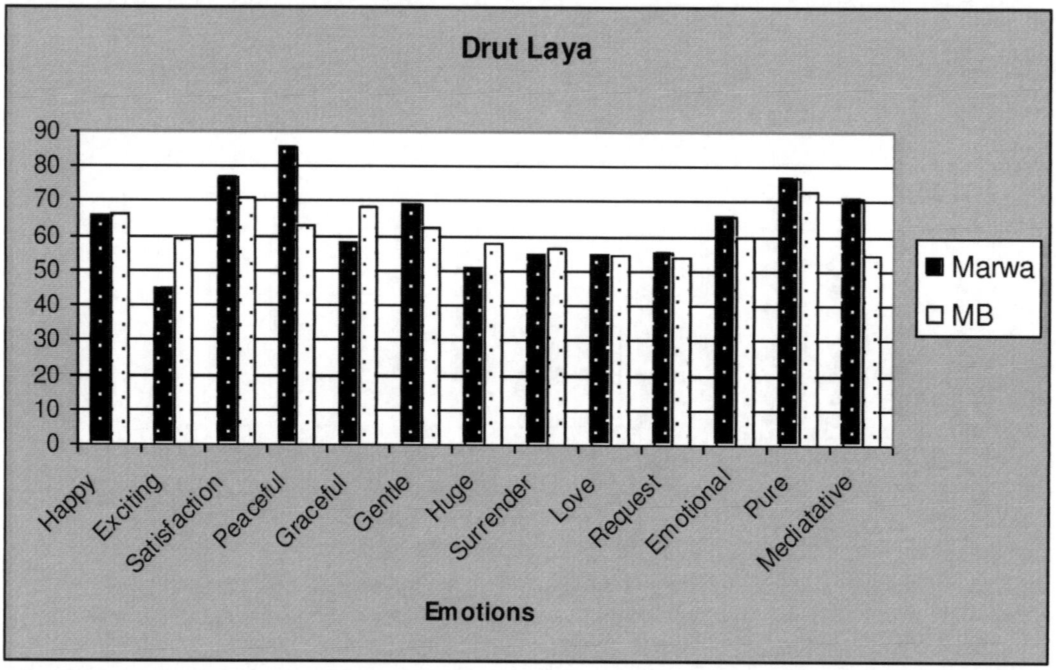
Drut Laya
90
80
70
60
50
40
30
20
10
0
Happy
Exciting
Satisfaction
Peaceful
Graceful
Gentle
Huge
Surrender
Love
Request
Emotional
Pure
Mediatative
Emotions
Marwa
MB

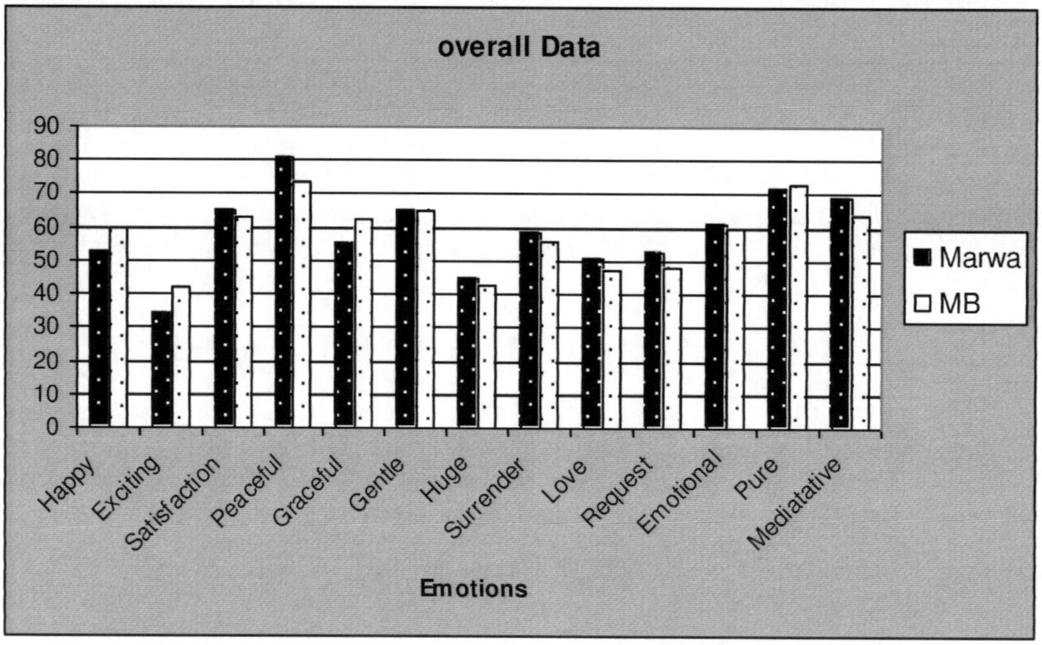
overall Data
90
80
70
60
50
40
30
20
10
0
Happy
Exciting
Satisfaction
Peaceful
Graceful
Gentle
Huge
Surrender
Love
Request
Emotional
Pure
Mediatative
Emotions
Marwa
MB

Affect Proxies and Ontological Change: A Finance Case Study

Xiubo ZHANG[1] *Khurshid AHMAD*[1]
(1) Trinity College, Dublin
xizhang@tcd.ie, kahmad@scss.tcd.ie

ABSTRACT
Traditional sentiment analysis has been focusing on inference of the sentiment polarity using sentiment-bearing words. In this paper, we propose a new way of studying sentiment and capturing ontological changes in a domain specific context in the perspective of computational linguistics using affect proxies. We used Nexis service to create a domain specific corpus focusing on banking sectors. We then created an affect dictionary from three kinds of lexica: sentiment lexica as in the General Inquirer dictionary; news flow represented by domain entities such as financial regulators and banks; and what we call *contested* term lexica, which consists of terms whose semantic implication is inconsistent over time. Univariate and multivariate analysis techniques such as factor analysis are used to explore the relationships and underlying patterns among the three types of lexica. Analysis results suggest that citations of regulatory entities show strong correlation with negative sentiments in the banking context. Also, a factor analysis was conducted, which reveals several groups of variables in which the *contested* terms correlate with positive and negative sentiments.

KEYWORDS: sentiment analysis, affect proxy, computational linguistics, factor analysis, contested terms, ontological change.

1 An Introduction and the Case Study

In rapidly changing environments, for example the aftermath of the 2008 credit crunch, we saw the advent of US and EU economic and financial stabilization schemes, changes in the regulatory frameworks include major revisions of existing concepts (e.g. capital adequacy), introduction of new concepts (e.g. novel regulatory pathways), and constraints on existing concepts/practices (e.g. sub-prime loans). These changes are articulated in new or revised governmental legislation and voluntary codes of practice over a period of time – there are commentaries and interpretation of these changes. All these organisations produce prodigious quantities of documents on a daily or even hourly basis and broadcast the documents using data feeds and social media; there is a concomitant flow of new and revised keywords from the compliance and regulatory agencies.

The post credit squeeze language of the regulators and that of the regulated is suffused with negative affect – indeed the terms *credit squeeze, credit freeze, zombie loans/banks* are used to express the negative evaluation of the state of leading economies and their financial institutions. Times of change invariably involve the introduction of new terms, or more importantly old terms are retrofitted with new meanings or nuances. Indeed, the early pioneers of sentiment analysis, discussed the changing language of "American values" by an analysis of changes in the language of the two major political parties in the USA – the Democratic and the Republican parties (Namenwirth and Lasswell, 1970). The authors argue that the anti-slavery party (the Republicans) became less inclusive (compared to the Democrats). This claim was based on an analysis of "inclusivity" words in the election manifestos of the two parties between 1844-1864 and 1944-1964, the authors had used the General Inquirer system and the associated lexica (Stone, 1966). This text analytic approach suggests that major changes in the attitudes within a community can perhaps be discerned by examining the choice of words belonging to domain terms (political and economic) and the affect terms (negative/positive evaluation, strength and orientation). The question we ask in this paper is this: Are the changes in attitudes related to changes in the ontological commitments of the community (e.g. from pro-slavery to anti-slavery, from pro-federation to autonomous units in (Namenwirth and Lasswell, 1970)?.

Revert to the 2008 financial crisis: prior to the crisis, there was a vocal body of opinion that was in favour of *light-touch regulation*, and compliance and governance issues were expected to be dealt with within financial institutions. Things have changed considerably since 2008 what with the ever complex national and international compliance frameworks, direct governmental management of financial institutions, and a resurgence of regulators.

One iconic term which hallmarks the 2008 crisis is *light-touch regulation*: In the decade before the crisis, the banks, the regulators, and indeed the media and governments, wished for and implemented minimal (state) regulations, self-governance, and low-level of compliance, for the financial services industry. Things have changed after the decade and *light touch regulation* will be giving way to *abundant regulation*! A survey of associated sentiment with *light touch regulation* using Google search engine and selecting one of first 10 most relevant documents for the term sampled every two years from 2002 shows the contested nature of the headword – regulation. Furthermore, the affect terms associated with light touch regulation for sentiment evaluation changed polarity – from negative to positive (Table 1).

A large number of US government agencies and professional bodies, around 12 at the last count, are involved in (a) monitoring financial institutions for compliance with existing laws and codes of practice; (b) producing regulations and regulatory frameworks; and (c) examining

Date	Headline and Source	KWIC
18 Nov 2002	average banking cost* (euro/year) [British Bankers' Association]	Historically *light touch regulation* ... has driven banks to be more efficient
8 Jul 2004	House of Commons - International Development - Written Evidence	We welcome the principles of *light touch regulation* ...
4 Dec 2006	SELLING THE CITY SHORT? [Open Europe Think Tank]	Bermuda ... enjoy *light-touch regulation* ...
22 Jun 2006	Gordon Brown's Mansion House speech | Business [Guardian.co.uk]	... the future, advance with *light touch regulation*, a competitive tax environment ...
17 Oct 2008	The days of light-touch regulation in the City are over,' warns head ... [Daily Mail]	The City watchdog ... warned the days of *light-touch regulation* ... are over.
12 Mar 2010	(UK FSA) calls time on FSA's "light touch" regulation – [Telegraph]	(UK) will drop its long-held commitment to ... *"light-touch" regulation*
3 May 2012	Switzerland says goodbye to light touch regulation [Reuters. Blog]	Switzerland says goodbye to *light touch regulation* ...

Table 1: Changes in the polarity associated with a contested term light touch regulation between 2002-2012

the governance of financial institutions. In itself, the involvement of agencies in (a)-(c), appears a normal, routine matter in that business-critical institutions should by default comply with laws, have good regulatory framework, and demonstrate exemplary governance. The fact that concepts related to *compliance*, *governance* and *regulation* are still being contested in the media is an interesting manifestation of regulatory change from *light-touch regulation* and/or *self-regulation* to something else, e.g. *smart regulation*. The evidence of this continuing debate can be perhaps seen in news reports relating to the key financial institutions – the *banks* and its regulators.

It appears that a major shift in (inter-)national policies regarding an area of human enterprise, that is a major change in the ontological basis of the enterprise, is accompanied by changes in the use of domain specific terms including named entities in the domain, changes in evaluation of the domain specific terms through a change in associated affect terms, and changes in what we call *contested* terms. Contested terms generally include terms related to the basic operation of an enterprise. For instance, banks to have to comply with existing law, banks should have transparent governance structures, and banks have to be regulated well. But the question is to what extent and by whom: *lightly* by the banks themselves or *strictly* by the regulators.

It is important to note that affect can be expressed at three different levels pragmatic description: First, the number of news stories in a fixed interval of time can be used as a measure of affect evaluation – the so-called news flow is an important affect proxy. Second, the changes in the distribution of the contested terms can also be used as a proxy for changes in affect or sentiment. And, third, the distribution of the domain independent affect terms, if computed accurately and with appropriate degree of disambiguation, can be used as a more direct measure of sentiment.

All three measures of affect or sentiment, news flow and the distribution of the contested and evaluation (positive/negative affect) terms closely follow the boom and bust within the world economic system.

Sentiment analysis is an interdisciplinary enterprise involving computer scientist, linguists, literature experts, cognitive psychologist and domain experts. One can argue that sentiment

Banco Santander	BNP Paribas	Deutsche Bank	Mitsubishi UFJ
Standard Chartered	Bank of America	Citibank	Goldman Sachs
Mizuho Financial	State Street	Bank of China	Commerzbank
HSBC	Morgan Stanley	Sumitomo Mitsui	Bank of New York Mel.
Credit Agricole	ING	Nordea	UBS
Banque Populaire	Credit Suisse	J.P. Morgan Chase	RBS
UniCredit	Barclays	Deixa	Lloyds
Societe Generale	Wells Fargo		

Table 2: 30 named entities used in the corpus design

analysis encompasses computational linguistics and has psychologists and domain experts additionally. In this paper, we look at the analysis of sentiment by looking at dictionaries compiled by psychologists and linguists. We begin by describing the design and implementation of our corpus (c. 12 million words) and a specially designed lexica for dealing with affect and affect proxies in Section 2. This is followed by a description of the method we used. The results section comprises the results of univariate and multivariate analysis reported in Section 4 and then we conclude.

2 Design of the Corpus and *Affect* Lexica

2.1 Corpus Design

Our analysis is targeted on a corpus comprising news articles related to 30 major banks around the world as shown in Table 2. We have used the Nexis database of news and related documents to collect the bank-related news over an 11 year period (2001-2011); our choice of this news source was motivated by the availability of rich meta-level information that is used to annotate, and subsequently retrieve each news document in Nexis. Our data set contains 22 sub-corpora each comprising six months of news. For each of the six month period, a query is issued to search the articles using the bank names as keywords over a pre-defined set of sources called "Major World Newspapers (English)" within Nexis: the top 1000 most relevant articles returned by the search are retained. We did not restrict our search to a particular news paper because we believe the overall prospect of the banking sector might be better captured in a global perspective. Our use of the relevance metric provided by Nexis was motivated by the thought that the sampling process should remain consistent and largely free of any biases or framing during manual selection of media sources [1].

The meta-level information was extracted automatically from raw text downloaded from Nexis data base [2]. The information can be used to extract the date of publication and news source. The publication dates come with the documents allow us to aggregate the daily news stories into lower frequency data – weekly, monthly or yearly. The news source information help us to use all news from all sources or to dis-aggregate the news according to sources. The time period aggregation and news source dis-aggregation can help capture the effect of time scale or the news source.

[1] The duplication-removal option in Nexis was used, the actual amount of articles obtained per search is usually less than 1000, but as the occurrences of duplication can be regarded as random events, we believe the corpus created this way is consistent and representative.

[2] The raw documents downloaded are unstructured and a Java program was written to extract the meta-data annotation from the text, which contain the date on which the news was published as well as the source of the news.

Title	Articles	Tokens	Average Article Length
Year: 2001	1890	1157837	612.61
Year: 2002	1857	877891	472.75
Year: 2003	1794	846660	471.94
Year: 2004	1886	939377	498.08
Year: 2005	1593	1002570	629.36
Year: 2006	1953	1271229	650.91
Year: 2007	1918	1231522	642.09
Year: 2008	1879	1416622	753.92
Year: 2009	1771	1285902	726.09
Year: 2010	1791	1247322	696.44
Year: 2011	1797	1254569	698.15
Total	20129	12531501	
Mean	1830	1139227	622.94

Table 3: Yearly breakdown of the corpus

For the 30 banks, Nexis yielded 20129 relevant articles over the 10 year period, which enabled us to build a specialist corpus of 12.5 million words with a mean number of 1830 documents per year and an average length of 623 tokens (Table 3).

2.2 Lexica Design

Three lexica were used in our analysis:

2.2.1 Domain Lexica: The Financial Regulator / Banking Dictionary

The motivation behind the creation of this dictionary is the assumption that frequent mentions of financial regulators might imply the existence of inadequacy in regulatory enforcement, making the announcement of such agencies a proxy to negative sentiments. The dictionary contains 4 categories: US Regulators, UK Regulators, and Eurozone Regulators, with the fourth category containing a list of prominent banks, as nominated in (Forbes, 2011).

2.2.2 Affect Lexica: Harvard Dictionary of Affect

Harold Lasswell (Lasswell, 1948) has used sentiment to convey the idea of an attitude permeated by feeling rather than the undirected feeling itself. Such analyses of documents in the political and economic domain were boosted by the use large digitized dictionaries, notably the *GI Dictionary* also known as the *Harvard Dictionary of Affect* which formed the backbone for the *General Inquirer* system (Stone, 1966). The *GI Dictionary* currently comprises over 11,000 words. Each word in the Dictionary has one or more "tags". Some of these tags refer to the connotative meaning of the word, whilst others to its cognitive orientation, and some to the belongingness of the word to a specific domain. The words in the Dictionary have between one and 12 of the 128 "tags". These tags are divided into 28 or so categories.

The original, and linguistically rather dated *Harvard Dictionary of Affect*, has been used in our analysis purely for the evaluation affect words – negative and positive. Note that the *Harvard Dictionary* has affect tags associated with domain specific terms which can be misleading when an affect count is carried out. For example, *Harvard* has the word *competition* tagged as negative evaluation word, and the words *share* and *company* as positive evaluation words. This may

Keyword	Identity	Opposite	Remark
regulation	*control*		direct synonym of regulation
	supervision		synonym of synonym of control
		relinquishment	antonym of synonym of control
		disorganization	direct antonym of regulation
	coherence		antonym of antonym of disorganization
		dissolution	synonym of antonym of disorganization

Table 4: Semantic identity and opposition of the contested term *regulation*

have been true in everyday language of the 1940's and 50's (the times when the Dictionary was compiled), but today these words are used as keywords in the domains of economic and finance.

The system used in our analysis has been so designed that when a token from a given document is analyzed for its belongingness to affect categories, and if the token is found in a domain specific dictionary then the system ignores the affect category.

2.2.3 Contested Term Lexica

The contested terms lexica are a hybrid of domain specific terms and words in an affect lexicon. We use three ontological primitives – *compliance*, *governance* and *regulation* and populate the hybrid lexicon with synonyms and antonyms of each of the three primitives. The hypothesis we wish to test is the identity terms, especially synonyms of a given ontological primitive will reinforce messages related to the unit whilst the opposition terms, especially antonyms, will create a negative empr? of the primitive.

This population process can be accomplished by traversing a general thesaurus or a thesaurus similar to *WordNet* "intelligently" and to scrape data from synonymous and antonymous relationships between synsets as demonstrated in a variant of *WordNet* – *SentiWordNet* (Baccianella et al., 2010). For our study, we use a general language thesaurus that is freely available on-line at this time[3].

The dictionary is populated using an expansion algorithm, which starts with the three keywords, *governance*, *regulation* and *compliance*. The algorithm then iteratively populates the dictionary by assigning direct as well as indirect synonyms and antonyms of the three seed words to appropriate. An example expansion from the seed word "regulation" is shown in Table 4. The table demonstrates how the affect category *regulation identity* and *regulation opposition* are populated using synonyms and antonyms of the seed word regulation. A synonym of a word is considered to have the same affect evaluation as the word while an antonym of a word has the opposite affect evaluation. This rule is also applied iteratively to synonyms and antonyms of the seed word as well.

2.2.4 Merging Strategy

The above three dictionaries are merged together to form a single affect dictionary to be used in the analysis. After the merge, the set of categories to which a word belongs is the union of

[3]The thesaurus used in our study is an on-line thesaurus at *http://thesaurus.com*. Synonyms and antonyms that are shorter than four characters were excluded from the lexica to avoid common close-class words.

	Relationship	
	Identity	Opposites
Governance	337	34
Regulation	370	110
Compliance	185	291
Affect Evaluation	4923	6870

Table 5: Lexica statistics

the original three sets of categories the word is associated with. A summary of the statistics of the lexica is shown in Table 5.

3 Methodology

We employ a methodology similar to vector space model, where each document in the corpus is represented by a vector of N dimensions. The difference lies in the semantics of the space – the vectors measure affect strength rather than word frequency.

The merged dictionary created as described in Section 2.2 is used to transform documents to vectors. The dictionary is essentially a many-to-many mapping between words and dictionary categories, where each word in the dictionary is associated with one or more categories. The documents in the corpus are then converted into vectors where each element in a vector corresponds to the relative frequency of a specific affect category in that document.

The relative frequency of a category is computed as the sum of the absolute frequencies of words belonging to the category over the total number of words in the document. Formally, the strength of the category C in document D is given as Equation 1.

$$\text{AffectStrength}(C,D) = \frac{\Sigma_{d\in D}\,|\{w|w \in d \wedge w \in C\}|}{\Sigma_{d\in D}\,|\{w|w \in d\}|} \tag{1}$$

The next phase of the method is to aggregate the document vectors based on the time of publication of the document. Vectors that associate with documents from the same time period of interest are added together to form a single vector representing the affect characteristics of the specific period. The result of this aggregation is a multivariate time series. For our analysis, the documents are grouped into a monthly scale.

4 Analysis and Results

4.1 Univariate Analysis

4.1.1 News Flow

In text analytics in general, and in sentiment analysis in particular, news flow, typically number of relevant articles published in a given time interval, is used as a sentiment or affect proxy – see for instance Kim and Barnett's work in international marketing (Kim and Barnett, 1996), Cain's in political science (Cain, 2012), and Hafez and Xie's in finance (Hafez and Xie, 2012). A study of the aggregated monthly news flow in our corpus shows that the coverage of banks in news media during the three periods (c. 2001, 2002-2005, 2006-2011) is different: below the mean news flow in the boom period and above the mean during crises.

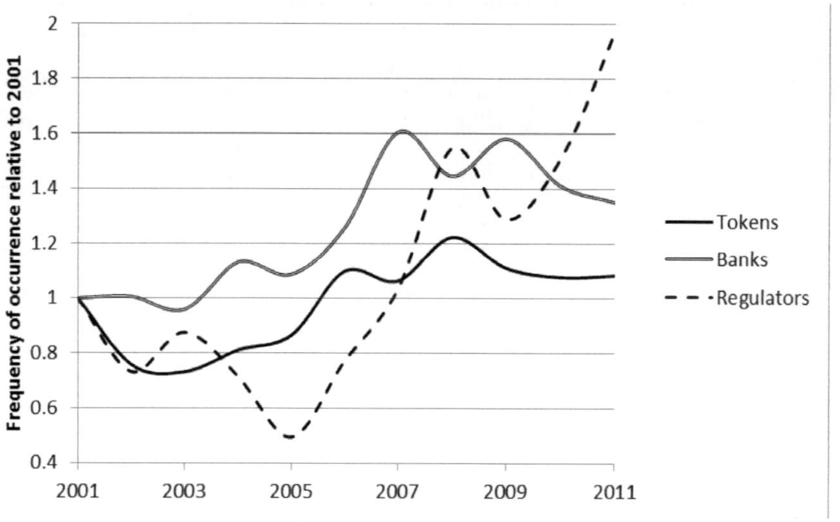

Figure 1: Annual frequency of total number of tokens and two named entities, banks and regulators, relative to 2001. (2001 frequencies – $N_{tokens} = 1157837$, $N_{banks} = 11326$, $N_{regulators} = 593$)

Three points to note here: (1) that following the dotcom boom (c. 2001) and until the first signs of the credit crunch (c. 2007), the yearly average word count, 500 tokens/news story, was much lower when compared with the pre-dotcom period, c. 600 tokens/news story, and the post boom period (c. 700 tokens/news story 2008 – to date); 2) there was a significant increase on the average length of articles talking about banks starting from 2005 and again another boost around 2009. The increase in the average length of the article pertinent to banks might be a result of the shift of public attentions towards banking sector during the financial crisis. A further Augmented Dickey-Fuller test for unit root shows that the series is non-stationary, which implies such shift must be structural rather than by chance.

The average frequency of the domain primitives, banks and regulators, i.e. the use of the names of banks and the regulators, in our 12.5 million word corpus, is 1.25% and 0.06% respectively. The annual distribution of the total number of tokens in our corpus is similar to that of the frequency of use of bank related tokens – higher in bust periods and lower in the boom periods (Figure 1); this is not surprising in that the corpus was created using the names and abbreviations of banks listed in Table 2. However the asymmetry in the distribution of bank related tokens and regulator related tokens is interesting in the sense that regulator related terms showed a drop in pre-2005 period but then there is an almost linear increase in the citations of regulators. Overall there is a 2.61% per annum increase in the regulator-related tokens whereas that of banks is 1%; these increment figures were computed using the historical return of the frequencies (logarithm of the ratio of this year's frequency of usage over last year's).

4.1.2 Contested Term Flow

The average annual frequency of the tokens related to the contested terms, *compliance*, *governance* and *regulation*, is 0.12%, 0.71% and 0.23% respectively in our 12.5m token banking corpora. The peak usage of three terms was in 2004 (*compliance*), 2006 (*governance*) and 2008

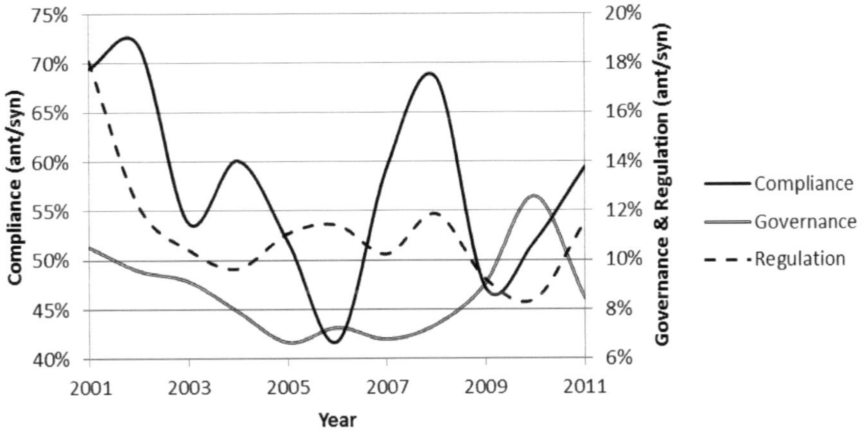

Figure 2: Annual frequency of total number of tokens and two named entities, banks and regulators, relative to 2001. (2001 frequencies – $N_{tokens} = 1157837$, $N_{banks} = 11326$, $N_{regulators} = 593$)

(*regulation*). The maximum usage of the three terms is within two standard deviation of the mean for each of three contested terms over the 10 years (2001-2011), showing a degree of stability of usage and perhaps our choice of the term and their synonyms and antonyms.

However, the distribution of the tokens related to synonyms and antonyms of the each of the contested terms is asymmetric, with synonyms being more widely used than the antonyms in each year of our observation. One can see the same effect in the language of general purposes: we have looked at the very broad coverage Google search engine and the more restricted American National Corpus (comprising 450 million words used in newspapers, fiction and other texts published during 1990-2012) and found a similar asymmetry in the distribution of a token and its antonyms.

What is interesting is the change in the asymmetry ratio over time: The average asymmetry for the compliance-related synonyms and antonyms is 58%, however, the maximum is around 70% (in 2002 and 2008) with a minimum of 40% in 2006. The ratio for the other two contested terms, *governance* and *regulation* is around 10% for every synonym used 10 times the antonym is used only once. The ratio again changes over our observation period (2001-2011) with a peak (18%) in 2002 (and minimum of 8% in 2012) for *regulation*. The asymmetry ratio for *governance* has a peak (13%) in 2010 (and a minimum of around 6% in 2005). The term compliance appears to be more contested than the other two (Figure 2).

4.1.3 Sentiment Flow

Typically, in financial studies, the negative sentiment has been found to be the causal variable that impacts the return on investment: Tetlock and colleagues have looked at a restricted set of tokens associated with negative affect and found a correlation between the variance in the frequency of such tokens and risk on the return. The author has argued that "high values of media pessimism induce downward pressure on market prices" (Tetlock, 2007): by media he means a financial gossip column in the Wall Street Journal and market "prices" refers to the logarithmic return of the daily values Dow-Jones Industrial Average Index. Elsewhere, we have noted that the historical volatility (proxied as standard deviation) of a negative affect time series (Devitt and Ahmad, 2008).

We have looked at the annual frequency distribution of the negative and positive affect tokens in our corpus, together with the logarithmic value of the ratio of the frequency of the current year and the previous year – usually called return. The asymmetry of the average value of the relative frequency, over the 10 years of our coverage, for negative and positive affect is 2:3, the values over the 10 year period for both affect series is within two standard deviation of the mean. However, the average value of return is 0.1% for negative affect but -0.02% for the positive affect: the volatility for negative affect is 5% whereas for positive affect 2% only. The differences are even starker when we divide the series of affect values in "boom" years (2002-2006) and "bust" period (2007-2011). The negative affect decreases overall in the boom period and vice-versa for the positive affect; contrariwise is the case for the bust period. The volatility of negative sentiment is much higher in the bust period.

4.2 Multivariate Analysis

The variables we have discussed thus far in the context of changing nature of(world-wide) financial systems dealt with three inter-related categories of tokens: domain specific tokens, contested tokens, and affect tokens. We have chosen to study not only the tokens but have constructed a polar space where we have (a) banks and their regulators; and (b) not only we have looked at contested issues, compliance, governance and regulations, but also at the identities and opposites of these tokens. In this section we will look briefly at the correlation between the distribution of the terms and attempt to identify combinations of these categories account for the variance of frequency distribution of tokens within the categories.

4.2.1 Correlation Analysis

We have looked at the correlations between the three categories of tokens and correlations across the categories. Correlations at 99% significance level appear between (a) negative affect tokens and (synonyms of) regulators, the correlation is positive, and (synonyms) of compliance anti-correlate with negative affect; positive affect tokens correlate with (synonyms of) governance and 90% significance level with the identities of compliance and regulation; (b) the frequency distribution of regulators is correlated with compliance; (c) the identity and opposites of compliance are positively correlated as are those of governance; the latter is correlated with the synonyms of regulation. (See Table 6 for details).

4.2.2 Factor Analysis

Pair-wise correlations in some cases help to identify relationships between two variables. However, the method makes it somehow difficult for human to gain insight into data, especially in terms of relationships between groups of variables. To obtain a better understanding of the overall picture between the variables, we performed a factor analysis on the data to explore latent patterns that may dictate the observed behaviors of the affect categories[4]. Factor analysis was initially developed in the discipline of psychology as a statistical approach to explain correlated variables using reduced number of "factors". In our study, we are mainly interested in its capability of grouping variables so that they can be better understood.

[4]The principal component analysis and factor analysis was done using Minitab 16.

			Affect		Domain		Contested					
			Negativ	Positiv	Banks	Regulators	Compliance		Governance		Regulation	
							Iden.[a]	Oppos.[b]	Iden.	Oppos.	Iden.	Oppos.
Affect	Negative		-									
	Positive		-0.039	-								
Domain	Regulators		0.543***	0.172**	-							
	Banks		0.033	-0.047**	-0.026	-						
Contested	Compliance	Iden.	-0.325***	0.175**	0.062	-0.266***	-					
		Oppos.	-0.089	0.036	0.061	-0.210**	0.322***	-				
	Domain	Iden.	-0.069	0.290***	0.165***	-0.017	0.188**	0.210**	-			
		Oppos.	-0.032	-0.092	-0.065	0.112	-0.106	-0.207**	-0.275***	-		
	Regulation	Iden.	0.062	0.212**	0.158*	0.011	-0.032	0.186**	0.288***	-0.013	-	
		Oppos.	0.190**	-0.139*	-0.019	0.060	-0.127*	0.115	0.198**	-0.081	0.142*	-

[a] Identity
[b] Opposite
*** $p \leq 0.01$
** $p \leq 0.05$
* $p \leq 0.15$

Table 6: Pair-wise correlation matrix and associated correlation significance

Variable	Factor1	Factor2	Factor3	Factor4	Factor5	Communality
Negativ	-0.83	0.00	0.14	-0.12	-0.06	0.72
Regulators	-0.82	-0.08	-0.07	0.02	0.09	0.69
compliance+[a]	0.58	-0.21	-0.18	-0.34	0.05	0.53
Positiv	0.02	-0.75	-0.42	-0.10	-0.06	0.75
regulation+	-0.01	-0.68	0.40	0.27	-0.16	0.73
governance+	0.06	-0.65	0.21	-0.37	-0.04	0.61
regulation-[b]	-0.17	-0.03	0.81	-0.08	0.05	0.69
compliance-	0.40	-0.18	0.42	-0.38	-0.04	0.51
governance-	0.01	0.04	-0.07	0.86	0.06	0.75
Banks	0.01	-0.12	-0.04	-0.06	-0.98	0.98
Variance	1.87	1.55	1.27	1.25	1.01	6.94
Var	0.19	0.16	0.13	0.13	0.10	0.69

[a] "+" denotes "identity"
[b] "-" denotes "opposition"

Table 7: Factor loadings from factor analysis

Firstly, a principal component analysis was carried in an attempt to determine the number of factors that would appear in the factor analysis. The result indicates that the first five factors combined explain 69 % of the variances, while the contribution of including the sixth factor is negligible. The factor analysis was then carried out using 5 factors on 10 variables: two variables each for both affect and the domain categories and two for each of the three contested token categories. The resulting factor loadings are rotated using Varimax Rotation for better interpretability. A total of 69% of the variances are explained by a combination of five factors as expected from the previous principal component anlaysis. The variables are explained fairly well, with seven of them having more than 65% of their variances explained by the factors (Table 7).

We then tried to interpret the factors by labelling them with semantic descriptions.

Compliance Factor *compliance+*[5], *compliance-*, *Negativ* and *Regulators* all have strong loadings on Factor 1, where compliance topics load to the opposite of Negative sentiment and regulator references. This conforms to what we observed in the correlation matrix in the previous section, where *Negativ* positively correlates with regulators and the compliance terms negatively correlates with *Negativ* as well as references to regulators. We suggest that this factor to be labeled as "Compliance Factor".

Positive Factor *regulation+*, *governance+* and *Positiv*, as we can see from the factor loading table, load heavily on Factor 2. Considering the supporting nature of the *regulation+* and *governance+* variables, we believe it makes sense to label Factor 2 as "Positive Factor".

Regulation Factor Factor 3 loads heavily on regulation, *regulation-* together with *compliance-*, and to the opposite of *Positiv* category. This could suggest that Factor 3 is related to the concept of regulation and compliance, while the concept generally occurs in a non-positive context. Therefore we suggest that Factor 3 be labeled as "Regulation Factor".

[5] *compliance+* denotes the identity concepts of *compliance* while *compliance-* denotes the opposition concepts of *compliance*. The same notion is applied to *governance* and *governance* to keep things concise.

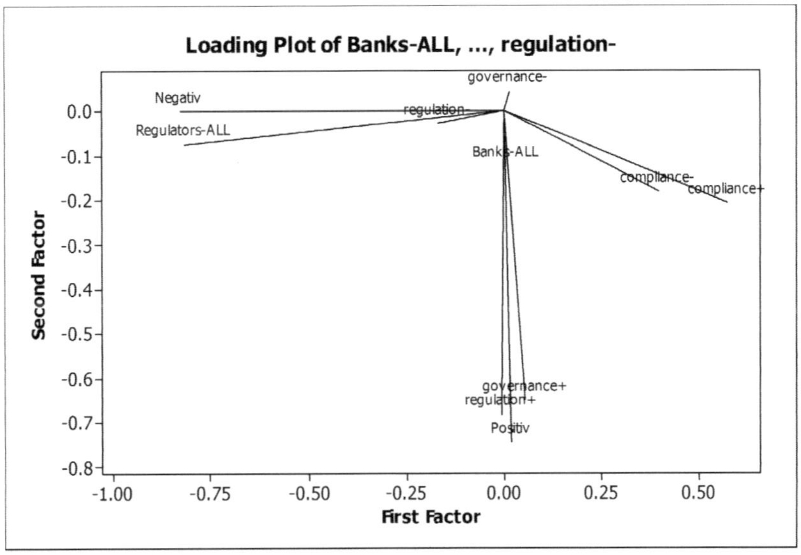

Figure 3: Factor loading plot

Cluster No.	Variables
1	*Banks-ALL*
2	*Negativ, Regulators-ALL*
3	*Positiv, compliance+, compliance-, governance+, regulation+*
4	*governance-*
5	*regulation-*

Table 8: Variable clusters

Governance Factor The category of *governance+* predominates Factor 4. The *governance-* category, however, loads to the opposite of *governance+*. This suggests that the discussions of governance are polarized – the contexts where governance are mentioned are either supportive or non-supportive of the governance concept. Therefore, we suggest that the Factor 4 be labeled as "Governance Factor".

Bank Factor Factor 5 is almost entirely dedicated to the citations to banks, hence we named it "Bank Factor".

Figure 3 shows the plot of the variables against the top two factors that explained the variances most, giving an intuitive representation of the distribution of the loadings. It can be seen fairly easily that the variables form three clusters. Following this intuition, we conducted a further analysis in which the variables are clustered according to their correlations[6]. Five clusters are identified and reported in Table 8.

It is worth noting that factor analysis only reveals correlations rather than casual relationships between the variables. In our case, the factors could be interpreted in two different ways. First, it could be argued that the sentiment variables are the "consequences" while the domain ones

[6]The analysis is performed using Minitab 16's "Cluster Variables" function.

are the "causes". For instance, in Factor 1, it might be reasonable to say that the contexts in which the regulators were cited are mostly negative in sentiment. This interpretation conforms with the conventional expectation from sentiment analyses, where we learn about the polarity of opinions with regard to certain topics. The second perspective of seeing the factors are to think the domain and contested variables as "proxies" or "indicators" of sentiment. Again, for Factor 1, it may be inferred that excessive citations of financial regulators indicates there is something "wrong" with the banking sector (thus negative).

Conclusion

In this paper, we proposed a hypothesis that the usages of domain entities (*financial regulators* and *banks*) and contested terms (terms relating to concepts that had bear much debate) could serve as proxies of ontological shifts in the general sentiment of the news in financial sectors.

We use a bag-of-words method for analyzing texts for computing the affect content. A univariate analysis of the distribution of three different types of terms in a large corpus of news about banks shows that the general level of negativity in the news about banks has increased. A multivariate analysis, based on correlation and factor decomposition, shows references to *regulatory bodies* strongly associated with *negative affect*, forming a heavily loaded factor in the analysis. We believe this might be strong evidence supporting our argument that those terms other than pure sentiment bearing words, for example, news flow and contested terms could possibly serve as proxies to sentiments in domain context. This, perhaps, is due to the fact that frequent discussions about a domain concept such as regulators or fierce debate over a contested term might imply the absence of such concept, which, in our case, is the regulation of the financial institutions. We have identified several other factors which could provide further insight to the relationships between contested terms and sentiments: a "positive" factor which also loads with pro-governance and pro-regulation terms; an anti-compliance and anti-regulation factor that has opposite loadings on positivity; an anti-governance factor, and a bank factor. Interpretation of the factors were attempted.

Our future work would focus on the refinement of contested term lexicon as well as exploring techniques from time series analysis to model the changes of news flow, contested terms and sentiments, which would help capturing the dynamics of the system better. We also plan to leverage lexical information more in the future to enhance the accuracy of analysis.

Acknowledgments

Thanks to Yorick Wilks for comments and advice on this research. This work was supported by Enterprise Ireland grant #CC-2011-2601-B for the GRCTC project and a Trinity College research studentship to the first author.

References

Baccianella, S., Esuli, A., and Sebastiani, F. (2010). SentiWordNet 3.0: An Enhanced Lexical Resource for Sentiment Analysis and Opinion Mining. In Chair, N. C. C., Choukri, K., Maegaard, B., Mariani, J., Odijk, J., Piperidis, S., Rosner, M., and Tapias, D., editors, *Proceedings of the Seventh conference on International Language Resources and Evaluation LREC10*, volume 25, page 2010. European Language Resources Association (ELRA).

Cain, G. (2012). How Can an Information Campaign Win Support for Peacekeeping? *Journal of International Peacekeeping*, 16(1-2):1–2.

Devitt, A. and Ahmad, K. (2008). Sentiment Analysis and the Use of Extrinsic Datasets in Evaluation. In *Proc. of the 6th Intl. Conf on Language Resources and Evaluation*.

Forbes (2011). World's Most Important Banks.

Hafez, P. and Xie, J. (2012). Factoring Sentiment Risk into Quant Models. *Available at SSRN*.

Kim, K. and Barnett, G. A. (1996). The Determinants of International News Flow A Network Analysis. *Communication Research*, 23(3):323–352.

Lasswell, H. D. (1948). The Structure and Function of Communication in Society. *The communication of ideas*, 37.

Namenwirth, J. Z. and Lasswell, H. D. (1970). *The Changing Language of American Values: a Computer Study of Selected Party Platforms*. Sage Publications.

Osgood, C. E., Suci, G. J., and Tannenbaum, P. (1967). *The Measurement of Meaning*, volume 47. University of Illinois Press.

Stone, P. J. (1966). *The General Inquirer: A Computer Approach to Content Analysis*. M.I.T. Press; First Edition edition (January 1, 1966).

Tetlock, P. C. (2007). Giving Content to Investor Sentiment: The Role of Media in the Stock Market. *The Journal of Finance*, 62(3):1139–1168.

Rule-Based Sentiment Analysis in Narrow Domain: Detecting Sentiment in Daily Horoscopes Using *Sentiscope*

Željko AGIĆ[1] *Danijela MERKLER*[2]
(1) Department of Information and Communication Sciences
(2) Department of Linguistics
Faculty of Humanities and Social Sciences, University of Zagreb
Ivana Lučića 3, 10000 Zagreb, Croatia
{zagic,dmerkler}@ffzg.hr

ABSTRACT
We present a prototype system — named *Sentiscope* — for collecting daily horoscopes from online news portals written in Croatian, detecting polarity phrases and overall sentiment conveyed by these texts and providing sentiment-analysis-based visualizations in a graphical user interface on the web. The system was evaluated using a dataset of daily horoscopes which was manually annotated for (positive and negative) polarity phrases and (positive, negative and neutral) overall sentiment. Linearly weighted kappa coefficient of 0.593 has indicated moderate inter-annotator agreement on overall sentiment annotation. The system achieved an F_1-score of 0.566 on overall sentiment and 0.402 on phrase detection. An overview of implementation is provided — with special emphasis on the polarity phrase detection module implemented in NooJ linguistic IDE — and the system is made available to users on the web.

TITLE AND ABSTRACT IN CROATIAN

Analiza sentimenata pravilima u uskoj domeni: pronalaženje sentimenata u dnevnom horoskopu sustavom *Sentiscope*

Predstavljamo prototip sustava — nazvanoga *Sentiscope* — za prikupljanje dnevnih horoskopa s novinskih internetskih portala pisanih hrvatskim jezikom, pronalaženje polarnih izraza i ukupnih sentimenata prenesenih tim tekstovima i pružanje skupa vizualizacija zasnovanih na analizi sentimenata putem internetskoga grafičkog korisničkog sučelja. Sustav je vrjednovan s pomoću skupa dnevnih horoskopa u kojima su ručno označeni (pozitivni i negativni) polarni izrazi i (pozitivni, negativni i neutralni) ukupni sentimenti. Linearni je *kappa*-koeficijent od 0.593 ukazao na umjereno slaganje označitelja pri označavanju ukupnoga sentimenta. Točnost je sustava izražena F_1-mjerom od 0.566 pri pronalaženju ukupnoga sentimenta i 0.402 pri pronalaženju polarnih izraza. Dan je pregled izvedbe sustava — s posebnim naglaskom na modulu za pronalaženje polarnih izraza izrađenom s pomoću lingvističkoga razvojnog okruženja NooJ — i korisnicima je omogućen internetski pristup sustavu.

KEYWORDS: sentiment analysis, narrow domain, rule-based system.

KEYWORDS IN CROATIAN: analiza sentimenata, uska domena, sustav temeljen na pravilima.

1 Introduction and related work

Sentiscope is a prototype system for sentiment analysis in daily horoscopes written in Croatian. It crawls the Croatian web on a daily basis and collects horoscope texts from several specialized websites and daily news portals. The texts are processed with a manually designed rule-based module for polarity phrase detection. The texts are then assigned with overall sentiment scores which are calculated by counting polarity phrases. The results of semantic processing are stored and the texts with the respective annotations of both polarity phrases and the overall sentiments are provided to users via a graphical user interface in the form of a web application.

Implementation of *Sentiscope* draws from the work on approaches to sentiment analysis in financial texts and related work on sentiment analysis presented in, e.g., (Ahmad et al., 2005, 2006a,b; Almas and Ahmad, 2007; Devitt and Ahmad, 2007, 2008; Daly et al., 2009; Remus et al., 2009). More specifically, drawing from the experiment with rule-based sentiment analysis in financial reports written in Croatian presented in (Agić et al., 2010) — which resulted with a high precision prototype system — and the previously mentioned work on rule-based sentiment analysis in general, we attempted to approach the problem of sentiment analysis in Croatian text from a very specific, narrow and expectedly difficultly processable genre, i.e., horoscope text from the web.

Alongside system implementation and evaluation, we emphasize the ambiguity of sentiment detection in general — end especially in narrow and ambiguous domains, represented here by horoscope text — by creating a manually annotated dataset of horoscopes and calculating inter-annotator agreement for the overall article sentiment manual annotation task. This special emphasis is motivated by previous explorations of properties of various sentiment analysis challenges, relating inter-annotator agreement and task difficulty, such as (Pang and Lee, 2008) and (Bruce and Wiebe, 1999; Wiebe et al., 1999, 2004; Shanahan et al., 2006). For example, it is specifically stated by (Pang and Lee, 2008) that "different researchers express different opinions about whether distinguishing between subjective and objective language is difficult for humans in the general case." They also state that "for example, (Kim and Hovy, 2006) note that human annotators often disagreed on whether a belief statement was or was not an opinion while other researchers have found inter-annotator agreement rates in various types of subjectivity classification tasks to be satisfactory." Here we implicitly address the relation between difficulty of manual sentiment annotation and meaningfulness of tackling the same annotation problem algorithmically. Moreover, following (Riloff et al., 2003; Wiebe, 2000; Wilson et al., 2005), we investigate the role of certain parts of speech — such as adjectives, adverbs, nouns and verbs — in detecting different classes of polarity phrases.

In the following sections, we describe the system implementation and evaluation on the tasks of detecting polarity phrases and detecting overall article sentiment. The system prototype is available on the web (http://lt.ffzg.hr/sentiscope/).

2 System implementation

System overview is given in Figure 1 (left side). The system is basically a web- and Linux-based application built by open source technologies and it consists of four main components:

1. the focused web crawler written in PHP that collects and stores horoscopes from a number of Croatian horoscope and daily news portals,

2. the rule-based sentiment detector that detects positive and negative polarity phrases

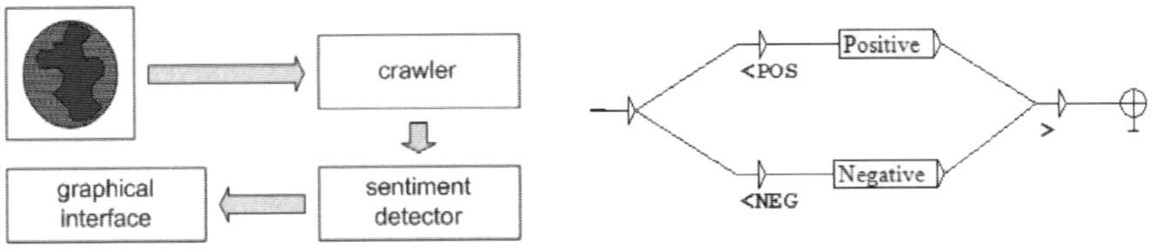

Figure 1: System overview and main polarity phrase detection grammar

Figure 2: Screenshot of the user interface

in horoscope text and is implemented as a set of local grammars designed in the NooJ linguistic development environment (Silberztein, 2004, 2005),

3. overall sentiment detector written in PHP that estimates overall article sentiment, i.e., horoscope sentiment by counting positive and negative polarity phrases and

4. the graphical user interface for assessing sentiment-annotated daily horoscopes and sentiment statistics over periods of time, as illustrated by Figure 2 and 4.

All horoscopes, respective polarity phrase annotations and overall sentiment scores are stored in a MySQL database. The user interface currently provides daily horoscopes with in-line annotations for all twelve zodiac signs (see Figure 2) and historical data in the form of overall sentiment diagrams. Both visualizations also conveniently and entertainingly serve as indicators of sentiment inconsistencies across zodiac signs and web sources. However, regardless of the overall purpose (or purposelessness) of such texts, it is shown here that texts from the specific horoscope genre written in Croatian are very difficult to process with respect to sentiment annotation and thus deserving the given research focus.

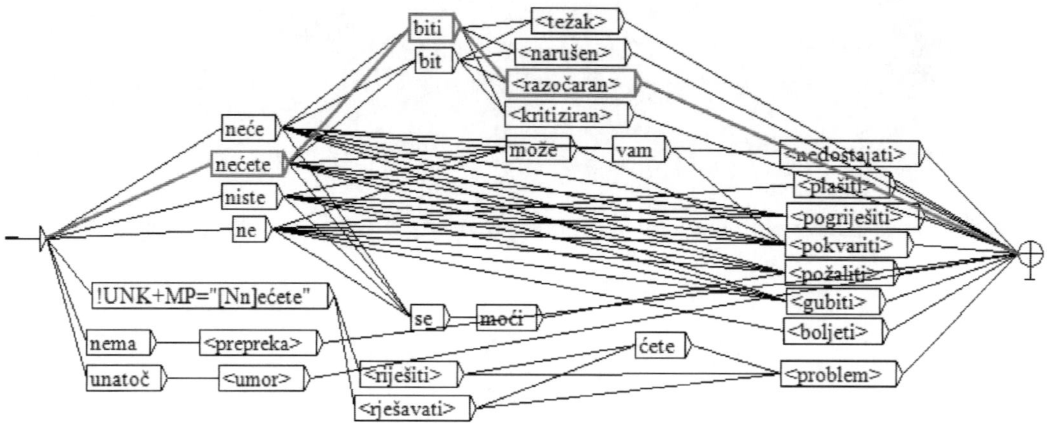

Figure 3: Example of positive polarity phrase detection using NooJ local grammars — hr. *nećete biti razočarani* (en. *you will not be disappointed*)

As mentioned previously, overall article sentiment is estimated from the number of detected phrases denoting positive or negative sentiment. Currently, articles are tagged as positive if the number of positive phrases is greater than the number of negative phrases contained within them and vice versa. If their counts are equal, the article is tagged as neutral. Polarity phrase detection is done by using a series of rules in form of local grammars or lexical finite state transducer cascades implemented in NooJ linguistic development environment, as illustrated in Figure 3.

Rules were designed in two stages — first from scratch and then by observing a development set of horoscope texts. For development and testing, we have collected horoscopes from seven largest Croatian websites containing daily horoscopes as indicated by the Google search index. Horoscopes were collected from 2012-02-11 to 2012-05-10. 7,716 articles with 484,179 tokens were collected. 333 articles were chosen for the development set and were manually annotated for overall sentiment and polarity phrases. Observed agreement of 75.97% on overall sentiment annotation was measured between the two annotators. The kappa coefficient indicated good strength of this agreement (0.641), while the linearly weighted kappa coefficient (0.593) assessment indicated moderate agreement. The stats are given in Table 1 and they indicate that the disagreement between the annotators was distributed almost exclusively within the category of neutral sentiment articles. The annotators agreed on positive sentiment in 80.69% of the annotations, while the observed agreement was 82% on negative sentiment and 66.09% on neutral sentiment. If we were to entirely exclude the category of neutral sentiment from data in Table 1, the observed agreement would be 99.44% and the respective kappa coefficient would amount to 0.989 and thus represent very good agreement strength.

Table 2 emphasizes the relation between the polarity phrases detected in articles and the overall sentiment of the articles and as such, it is the theoretical baseline for building a system that estimates overall sentiment of text from the number and type of polarity phrases that it contains. The table shows that the positive sentiment articles tend to contain much more positive polarity phrases, as 71.80% of the positive polarity phrases was found in positive sentiment articles, as opposed to 3.33% in negative and 24.87% in neutral sentiment articles. The same was found to

	+	–	x	Σ
+	94	0	26	120
–	1	82	31	114
x	18	4	77	99
Σ	113	86	134	333

Table 1: Inter-annotator agreement on overall sentiment

	<p>	<n>	both	<p> in both	<n> in both
+	410	27	23	85	27
–	19	321	15	19	53
x	142	145	67	117	115

Table 2: Relation between overall article sentiment (+, –, x) and polarity phrases (<p>, <n>)

apply for negative polarity phrases as well: 65.11% of them were located in negative sentiment articles, 5.48% in positive sentiment articles and 29.41% in articles carrying neutral overall sentiment. This justified a system design in which polarity phrases are counted in articles and overall sentiment assigned from the polarity group with the highest count. In addition to this, Table 2 also shows the number of articles in which both positive and negative polarity phrases were observed (table column *both*), along with separate counts of positive and negative polarity phrases (table columns *<p> in both* and *<n> in both*) for these articles. The distribution further supports the system design, being that positive polarity phrases are once again predominant in positive sentiment articles (75.89% positive vs. 24.11% negative) and negative polarity phrases dominate in negative sentiment articles (73.61% negative vs. 26.39% positive) while they are almost evenly spread in neutral sentiment articles (50.43% positive vs. 49.57% negative).

Rules for polarity phrase detection are grouped in two NooJ local grammars — one for positive sentiment and one for negative sentiment detection (see Figure 1, right side). Each of these grammars consists of lists of words and phrases for three parts-of-speech: adjectives, nouns and verbs. Another part-of-speech generally considered important in sentiment analysis — adverbs — are included within adjectives, due to the specifics in Croatian morphology, i.e., the fact that many adverbs in Croatian are homographic with adjective forms in singular nominative case in neuter gender: e.g., *brzo dijete* (en. *fast child*) *brzo trči* (en. *runs fast*). Words and phrases are manually derived from a number of daily horoscopes and — except for the characteristic key words and key phrases for the horoscope domain — there is a number of domain independent words and phrases, e.g., *dobro* (en. *good*), *izvrsno* (en. *great*), *odlično* (en. *excellent*) for positive sentiment, and *loše* (en. *bad*), *slabo* (en. *weak*), *nedovoljno* (en. *unsatisfying*) for negative sentiment. We derived 170 words and phrases for negative and 139 words and phrases for positive sentiment detection. In addition to the lists of positive and negative sentiment phrases based on their POS, there is also an aggregate of words which express positive or negative sentiment in itself, but in context, they often occur with a negation, which results in expressing the opposite sentiment. In the rules, there are 33 negated positive and 17 negated negative words and phrases (an example grammar for detecting negated negative words and phrases is given in Figure 3), which adds up in a total of 203 words and phrases for negative sentiment detection and 146 words and phrases for positive sentiment detection.

sample	precision	recall	F_1-score
initial	0.371	0.283	0.321
development	0.435	0.469	0.451
test	0.413	0.393	0.402

Table 3: Polarity phrase detection accuracy of the rule-based component

	+*	–*	x*	precision	recall	F_1-score
+	40	3	17	0.677	0.666	0.671
–	2	25	17	0.555	0.568	0.561
x	17	17	30	0.468	0.468	0.468

Table 4: System accuracy on overall sentiment (+, –, x) detection and confusion matrix for overall sentiment assignment (+*, –* and x* represent assignments by the system)

3 Evaluation

The evaluation was conducted on a manually annotated held-out test set containing 11,500 tokens in 168 articles. The initial prototype of the polarity phrase detection module, that was designed from scratch in NooJ, was first evaluated on the test set in a form of a *dry run* test for purposes of further development. The results are given in Table 3 joint for positive and negative polarity phrases. The results of the dry run were shown to be rather low, with an F_1-score of only 0.321. The rules were thus tuned, as previously mentioned, by observing the development set and another two tests were performed with the improved rules — one on the development set itself and the other on the test set. These results are also given in Table 3 and they show an improvement over the baseline for both the development set and the test set. Being that horoscope texts are highly complex in terms of irregularities of phrases, i.e., showing rare re-occurrences of polarity phrases among texts from varying sources, these scores were considered to be a satisfactory entry point for overall article sentiment detection.

The results of system evaluation with respect to overall article sentiment are given in Table 4. The rows of the confusion matrix represent gold standard annotation while the columns present system annotation. The matrix clearly indicates that the system performance is high for the task of discriminating between positive and negative overall sentiment, while its accuracy steeply decreases upon inclusion of the neutral sentiment article category. This observation is also supported by the inter-annotator agreement and the data in Table 1 and 2. The correlation between the number of polarity phrases and overall sentiment given in Table 2 is clearly manifested in the evaluation results, being that the overall performance of the system is satisfactory even if the rule-based phrase detection module performance might be considered somewhat low in absolute terms, especially with respect to those obtained for, e.g., well-structured financial texts (Agić et al., 2010).

Table 4 also shows that positive words and phrases are more accurately detected than the negative ones — the observed difference in F_1-scores of the positive and negative phrase detection is as high as 0.11 in favor of the positive phrase detection. Considering that there are substantially more negative words and phrases in the rules for detection (203 vs. 146) and that there are also considerably more negated positive phrases than vice versa (33 vs. 17),

sign	web sources							+	–	x
aries	x	x	+	x	+	+	x	3	0	4
taurus	–	+	+	+	x	x	x	3	1	3
gemini	+	–	+	–	x	x	x	2	2	3
cancer	–	+	+	x	–	–	x	2	3	2
leo	x	x	x	–	–	x	–	0	3	4
virgo	–	+	+	+	x	+	–	4	2	1
libra	–	–	+	–	+	+	x	3	3	1
scorpio	x	+	x	–	x	–	–	1	3	3
sagittarius	+	+	x	–	–	–	x	2	3	2
capricorn	x	x	+	+	x	x	x	2	0	5
aquarius	+	–	x	–	+	–	+	3	3	1
pisces	+	+	+	+	x	x	x	4	0	3

Table 5: Horoscope sentiment by web source on 2012-05-18

we can conclude that in this type of texts, unlike positive sentiment which is expressed more clearly and explicitly, negative sentiment is often covert and masked with various modifiers and within very complex expressions where negations occur far from the positive word (e.g., in hr. *danas nećete imati baš dobar dan*, en. *you will not have such a good day today*), so they are very difficult to detect with the rules.

Table 5 is an illustration of the sentiment trend information provided by the system. As mentioned previously, the texts are processed on a daily basis and both the texts and the respective annotations are stored in a database. This enables graphical display of sentiment trend across text sources (websites) and text categories (zodiac signs). The table indicates that the overall horoscope sentiment is consistently inconsistent across the seven different web sources and — perhaps even more interestingly — that the possible consistencies might be observed only within single web sources, not respecting the zodiac signs. In the specific case of sentiment analysis in the narrow domain of daily horoscope texts, this might therefore support the claim that perhaps the most reliable sentiment detection feature is the daily sentiment of the text authors. Sentiment trend is more explicitly encoded in Figure 4, as it presents an illustration of a sentiment time series with respect to zodiac signs (top) and web sources of horoscope texts (bottom). Figures for all categories, i.e., zodiac signs, web sources and different time frames are available via the system web interface (http://lt.ffzg.hr/sentiscope/).

Conclusion and perspectives

Detecting text sentiment in a very specific and narrow domain such as daily horoscope texts has shown not to be trivial and easy to achieve, given that such texts are characterized both by specific and often very complex phrases and syntax and a particular, domain-dependent style, which can be specific for each individual author, as well. This considered, obtained F_1-score of 0.566 for overall system accuracy and 0.402 for phrase detection accuracy, with observed annotator agreement of 75.97% (kappa 0.641, linearly weighted kappa 0.593), are here regarded as satisfactory and useful.

For future work, obtained data — the collected texts, the system and the processing results — can be used for different types of linguistic analysis, e.g., discourse analysis and socio-linguistic

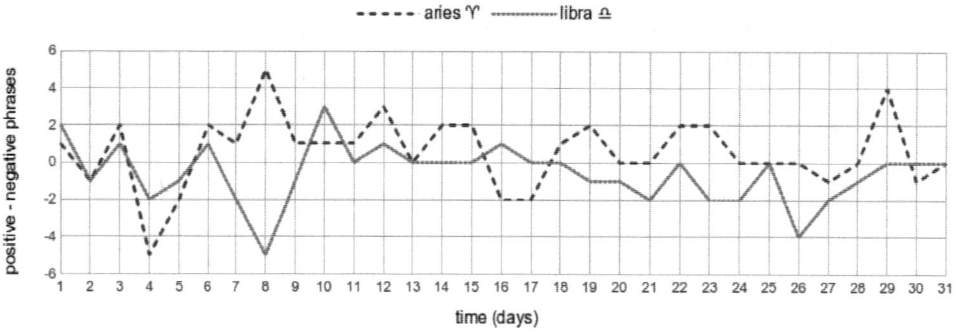

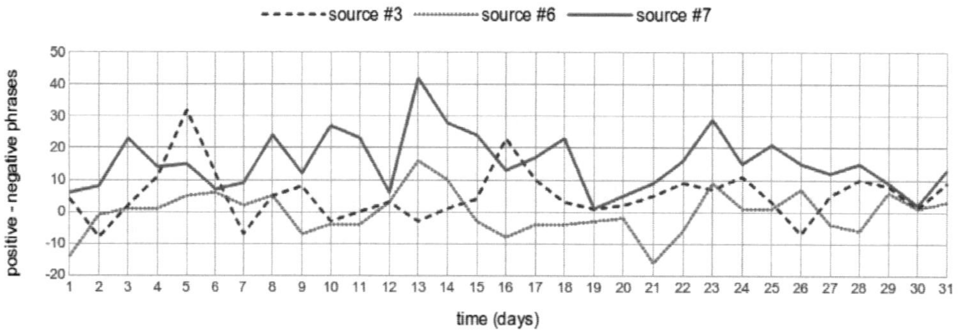

Figure 4: Overall sentiment time series by zodiac sign and web source for March 2012, expressed by the absolute difference between the number of detected positive and negative polarity phrases

analysis. Improvements to the implemented simple link between polarity phrases and overall sentiment might also be investigated, being that the current implementation trivially addresses (especially) neutral sentiment articles. Besides, the developed model could be easily adjusted and applied for sentiment annotation and visualization in other domains.

Acknowledgments

The presented results were partially obtained from research within project CESAR (ICT-PSP, grant 271022) funded by the European Commission, and partially from research within projects 130-1300646-0645 and 130-1300646-1776 funded by the Ministry of Science, Education and Sports of the Republic of Croatia.

References

Agić Ž, Ljubešić N, Tadić M. (2010). Towards Sentiment Analysis of Financial Texts in Croatian. In *Proceedings of LREC 2010*, ELRA, 2010, pp. 1164–1167.

Ahmad K, Gillam L, Cheng D. (2005). Society Grids. In *Proceedings of the UK e-Science All Hands Meeting*, Swindon, EPSRC, 2005, pp. 923–930.

Ahmad K, Gillam L, Cheng D. (2006). Sentiments on a Grid: Analysis of Streaming News and Views. In *Proceedings of LREC 2006*, ELRA, 2006.

Ahmad K, Cheng D, Almas Y. (2006). Multi-lingual Sentiment Analysis of Financial News Streams. In *Proceedings of the First International Conference on Grids in Finance*, International School for Advanced Studies, Trieste, Italy, 2006.

Almas Y, Ahmad K. (2007). A note on extracting "sentiments" in financial news in English, Arabic and Urdu. *The Second Workshop on Computational Approaches to Arabic Script-based Languages*, Linguistic Society of America, 2007, pp. 1–12.

Bruce R, Wiebe J. (1999). Recognizing Subjectivity: A Case Study of Manual Tagging. *Natural Language Engineering*, volume 5, 1999, pp. 187–205.

Daly N, Kearney C, Ahmad K. (2009). Correlating Market Movements With Consumer Confidence and Sentiments: A Longitudinal Study. *Text Mining Services*, Leipzeiger Beitrage zur Informatik, 2009, pp. 169–180.

Devitt A, Ahmad K. (2007). Sentiment Polarity Identification in Financial News: A Cohesion-based Approach. In *Proceedings of the Annual Meeting of the Association of Computational Linguistics (ACL 2007)*, Prague, Czech Republic, 2007.

Devitt A, Ahmad K. (2008). Sentiment Analysis and the Use of Extrinsic Datasets in Evaluation. In *Proceedings of LREC 2008*, ELRA, 2008.

Kim S-M, Hovy E. (2006). Identifying and Analyzing Judgment Opinions. In *Proceedings of HLT-NAACL*, 2006.

Pang B, Lee L. (2008). Opinion Mining and Sentiment Analysis. *Foundations and Trends in Information Retrieval*, volume 2, number 1-2, 2008, pp. 1–135.

Remus R, Heyer G, Ahmad K. (2009). Sentiment in German language news and blogs, and the DAX. *Text Mining Services*, Leipzeiger Beitrage zur Informatik, 2009, pp. 149–158.

Riloff E, Wiebe J, Wilson T. (2003). Learning Subjective Nouns using Extraction Pattern Bootstrapping. In *Proceedings of CoNLL*, 2003, pp. 25–32.

Shanahan J, Qu Y, Wiebe J. (2006). Computing Attitude and Affect in Text: Theory and Applications. *Information Retrieval Series*, number 20, Springer, 2006.

Silberztein M. (2004). NooJ: an Object-Oriented Approach. In *INTEX pour la Linguistique et le Traitement Automatique des Langues*, Cahiers de la MSH Ledoux, Presses Universitaires de Franche-Comté, pp. 359–369. See URL http://www.nooj4nlp.net/.

Silberztein M. (2005). NooJ's Dictionaries. In *Proceedings of the Second Language and Technology Conference*, Poznan University, 2005.

Wiebe J. (2000). Learning Subjective Adjectives from Corpora. In *Proceedings of AAAI*, 2000.

Wiebe J, Wilson T, Bruce R, Bell M, Martin M. (2004). Learning Subjective Language. *Computational Linguistics*, volume 30, number 3, 2004, pp. 277–308.

Wiebe J, Bruce R, O'Hara T. (1999). Development and Use of a Gold Standard Data Set for Subjectivity Classifications. In *Proceedings of the 37th ACL Conference*, 1999, pp. 246–253.

Wilson T, Wiebe J, Hoffmann P. (2005). Recognizing Contextual Polarity in Phrase-Level Sentiment Analysis. In *Proceedings of HLT/EMNLP*, 2005, pp. 347–354.

Author Index

Association for Computational Linguistics
209 N. Eighth Street
Stroudsburg, Pennsylvania 18360

CURRAN ASSOCIATES INC
proceedings.com

Sixth Workshop on Syntax, Semantics and Structure in Statistical Translation 2012

(SSST-6)

Held at the 50th Annual Meeting of the Association for Computational Linguistics (ACL 2012)

Jeju, Republic of Korea
12 July 2012

ISBN: 978-1-62748-345-2